Living by the Dead

the Dead

A MEMOIR

Praise for *Living by the Dead*...

"Life and death in a cemetery: This is a charming, brave, and funny book, with a sad heart." —Bailey White, regular NPR commentator, *Sleeping at the Starlite Motel, Mama Makes Up Her Mind, Quite a Year for Plums*

"This book about a cemetery seduces with delight—by turns moving, funny, bitter, inventive, melancholy, playful—until it delivers its last wrenching blow. Ellen Ashdown weaves the story of her family through the graveyard in which some of them are buried, and beside which she abides, bringing thoughtfully and finally heartbreakingly to life those who pass by, pass through, and pass on. Here is new proof that America abounds with first-rate writers who do not reach the imprints of New York and Boston. We must be grateful for literary presses like Kitsune Books for bringing them to print." —Janet Burroway, *Writing Fiction, Raw Silk, Cutting Stone, Opening Nights*, and forthcoming *Bridge of Sand*

"Ellen Ashdown's *Living by the Dead* is a compact, mesmerizing memoir more about life than death. Ashdown takes us like friends on her forays into Tallahassee's Roselawn Cemetery. It's Ashdown's observations on the blurry line between the living and the dead who, from the grave, give us some of the secrets of life." —Marina Brown, freelance writer, RN and Certified Hospice and Palliative Care Nurse

"Ellen Ashdown's moving memoir chronicles one woman's walk on the edges of life's great unknown—death. She and her husband move into a house near a cemetery that one by one takes those she loves. Yet she keeps observing with clear eyes and a heart that aches, yes, but never shuts itself off from the beauty that surrounds her. This is a luminous meditation on death but more than that an affirmation of the deep and quotidian glory of the world." —Barbara Hamby, *The Alphabet of Desire, Delirium, Babel*

"*Living by the Dead* is a book about life and memory—and walking through a cemetery. Writing with the soul of a poet and a ravenous curiosity, Ellen Ashdown interrogates the cemetery's stones and herself, wondering about the bluebirds or the raging grief that possesses her. Through the simple act of taking one step after another, Ashdown travels through her own inner journey of loss, grief, and love." —Sally Sommer, dance historian and critic, New York correspondent for *Le Monde*

Living by the Dead

A MEMOIR

Ellen Ashdown

Kitsune Books

Quality books for eclectic readers

Living by the Dead

Kitsune Books
P.O. Box 1154
Crawfordville, FL 32326-1154

www.kitsunebooks.com
contact@kitsunebooks.com

Printed in USA
First printing 2008

ISBN-13: 978-0-9792700-5-5

Library of Congress Control Number: 2008923484

Cover photo: Anne Petty
Back cover portrait: Beverly Frick
Map and chapter art: Mary Liz Tippin-Moody
Cover design: Anne Petty

Acknowledgements

My deepest gratitude is to the circle of family and friends who first read Living by the Dead and encouraged me to publish it. Always, as I wrote, I envisioned a map, which artist, colleague, and friend Mary Liz Moody so wonderfully brought to life. She involved herself personally in the places and story, generously created the chapter drawings, and immeasurably enriched the book.

I thank the keeper of Roselawn, Wayne Britt, for sharing a basic map of the cemetery's layout, but most of all for his basic humanity in every contact.

I thank photographer Beverly Frick for her personal warmth and aesthetic elegance. I thank copyeditor Lynn Holschuh for her expert eye and for still singing Gary's songs. Finally, I offer admiration and appreciation to Anne Petty, who wants to make books only because she loves them. I am just one beneficiary of her talent and drive, and of Kitsune Books.

For them all.

CONTENTS

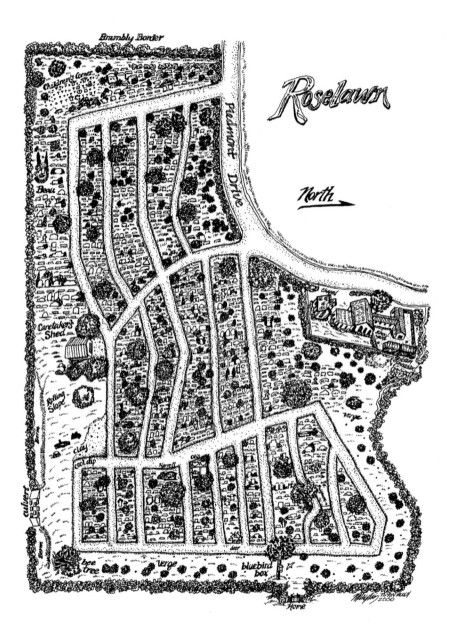

Roselawn

North →

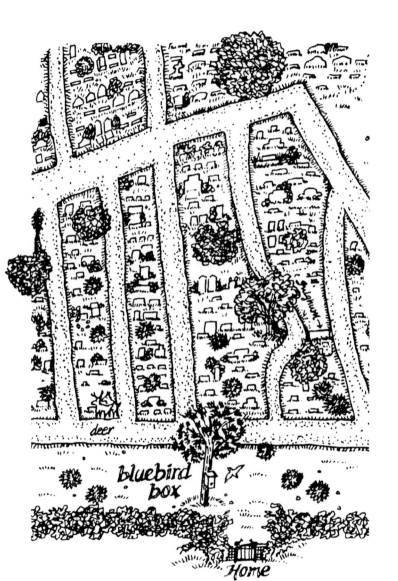

deer

bluebird
box

Home

CHAPTER 1

Speaking in Stones

The realtor made jokes about quiet neighbors. Gary and I made jokes about throwing each other over the back fence (when the time came). We weren't at all bothered by living in a house on a cemetery. After all: location, location, final location.

Gary and I, in truth, liked cemeteries. We toured them on holidays. Just when or why this semi-ghoulish habit began, I'm not sure, but the cemetery my memory has chosen as first was a Spanish-moss-draped archetype in Beaufort, South Carolina, barely above sea level. Some holidays are magic—true "holy days"—that transport you out of ordinary time, and Beaufort did this: New Year's Eve in the Deep South, dinner in an antebellum house, gray January days, foot-thick tabby walls, and time-stopped walks in a graveyard no one seemed to enter but us.

I found the grave of Charles Brockden Brown, America's first novelist. Or at least I believe I did. Brown's novel *Wieland* was a Gothic tale of madness, dissolution, and murder (much before Poe took over the territory), and if Brown isn't resting under the moss in Beaufort, he should be. I have somewhere, some time, stumbled upon his stone with a shock. South Carolina it now is.

Then there was Paris, where the elaborately crumbling homes of the dead are alive with cats. New Orleans, its filigreed younger sister. Vermont, where a dozen very old markers (by New World standards, of course) spring up in every few twists of tortuous roads

Cemeteries are set apart. Not forbidding, really; not always beautiful; but separate. And still. And Gary and I wanted the quiet. We were leaving a house on a busy thoroughfare, two blocks from a hospital and a few more from the fire department. We loved the house, our first, but we were ready to go.

Yet the quiet neighbors we would have at the new house weren't all strangers. The ashes of my mother, my brother, and my father rested there, and I hoped the euphemism was true, because after the horror of their deaths—three individual horrors—they deserved rest.

Gary said nothing. I said nothing. We set a date for closing. One night, quietly, he looked at me and said, "Ellen, will you be all right?" I did not say, "What do you mean?" I was waiting for the question, though I had not known it, and with the asking, I could say, truthfully, "Yes."

Trumpeted

Besides, as I soon discovered, my family had some decidedly lively neighbors, even flamboyant. All was not gloom and melancholy in roseless Roselawn, where I began to walk regularly and do still. Gentle hills, shade and sun, huge oaks and pines, glorious camellias and dogwoods, a one-mile circumference with winding inner roads: why didn't our neighbors walk here too? Instead, the Geezer Parade (Gary's christening) marched by our front door. One loop around our block was a half mile, and loop and loop the retirees did. Meanwhile, I had my backyard cemetery almost to myself.

I did share Otis with friends. Otis was the resident partner, waiting patiently for his wife Vera in their elaborate pink granite doublewide. Mom-and-Pop gravestones were new to me. In this conjugal tradition, when the first spouse dies, both spouses' names are engraved on one headstone; all that's wanting is a completing date (and body) for the survivor. This is commitment, surely, but how did Vera feel, visiting her dear husband's grave and seeing herself already there (a name, if not a foot, in the grave)?

Proud. The Wallace site is not so much a monument as a declaration: "Looky here at us!" Two thick pink slabs cover the graves themselves (twin beds, so to speak) and are connected to the double headstone-headboard. And oh my, there is so much to looky at. Working down from the top:

A cross.

Two huge carved hearts, one for Otis and one for

Vera, with dates and praying hands inscribed.

Linked wedding bands proclaiming "Married August 3, 1943."

A color photograph of the couple, printed on plastic and mounted between the hearts, with the sentiment, "Always together forever with Christ in Heaven."

Finally, at the base, between two flanking, W-monogrammed flower urns:

DADDY   WALLACE   MAMA

Note: we haven't reached the slabs yet. There, on Daddy's side, is what I really bring my friends to see. Not just the engraved, brightly colored dagger, sickle moon, and star. No, the bus. The Trailways bus. It's quite a good likeness, really: deeply etched into the slab, nicely colored, realistically foreshortened, its destination blazoned above the front windshield: Heaven. Where else?

We showed Otis to more than one group of friends and family. After a moment's silence, someone usually states the obvious, "He must have been a bus driver," and a wit adds, "Or been hit by one."

The whole display is incomparably gaudy. We marvel. We laugh. But Otis and Vera and their five children (whose names are written on the back of the headstone) slowly became more real to me—even before the day I saw three grown children paying their respects to Daddy. I kept my distance. For some reason, though curious, I didn't want to see them well.

Well, I do know the reason—more than one. Respect. A presumptuous fondness for the whole Wallace clan, who so clearly honored their father. An instinctive, perhaps selfish, desire to keep them mythical, shadowy.

The Wallace family have created a sanctuary, according to their lights. I saw one day that it is beautiful. They've planted crape myrtles, which now flourish and, each mid-summer, encircle the pastel stone in flowered branches of a duskier pink.

They've installed a bench. Perhaps Vera sits there many times when I am at home, enclosed in my brick walls as Otis is in his granite ones. I have had to recognize that the cemetery exists even when I'm not in it. But I don't think the bench is often used. More symbolic than practical, graveside benches—almost always empty—still whisper, "Someone sits here with you."

Otis wins the cemetery's novelty prize hands down, but close by is a neighbor who may have been as showy in life as he is in death. This is Carol, "The Lady in Red." I suspect that even for Carol (and those who buried her) a red gravestone seemed *outré*. They chose black, carved in its surface a large-brimmed hat with flowing ribbons, and gave her the cemetery's sexiest epithet. She died at sixty. Is her grave zestful or brave or sad or all? I think of her as unmarried; I know her to be bold. Think of it: How many women are known for extravagant hats and the color red? How many, at sixty, set such emblems in stone, in perpetuity—or inspire others to do so? The power and the glory to you, Carol, sad or sure.

No cryptic hints of mystery for Tony Harrell, though. His stone is his life, and his name is his image. Crowded with the colorful icons of a life cut short, his monument is like Egyptian pictorial biography. An artist has transformed the letters *T O N Y H A R R E L L* into the torso of the young man (thirty-two), seated at his desk at the Florida Department of Environmental Regulation. In this iconography, blessed are the bureaucrats. I think of the Florida governor who once called lazy state workers "lard bricks." Tony Harrell, forever solidified on the job, took the brick part of the insult very much to heart.

However, he's not working. He's reading the *Tallahassee Democrat*. Other signs that Tony Harrell wasn't a complete workaholic abound. A basketball, bat, baseball, and bicycle show his sports preferences. Perhaps he played at the University of Illinois, the school displayed on his diploma. Or maybe for a church league. Is that why "First Baptist Church" appears on a pennant, not on a Bible or cross?

The spines of the three books on his bookshelf are labelled "Engineering, Sports, Computers." Besides these loves, we know he loved Terri, whose name is enshrined in a heart. She is his wife, Harriet. On the other side of the headstone, she pledges her name to him formally, eternally, like Otis's Vera. But Terri is so young. Terri and Tony. At first I thought they had no children, weren't ready for them. Then I found "Annie" and "Matthew" written and drawn in the photo frame.

Of course there were children. This was a man building a world around him. Work, family, religion, recreation. He couldn't hold it, they couldn't hold it, but Terri has tried. She is probably nearing forty now. Every odd and loving detail on this headstone blazons her anguish when her husband died. But will she lie beside him in another forty years? Would he want her to? The world doesn't stop when someone dies; we just feel it should.

Probably no other headstone in Roselawn tries so

completely to capture, and publish, an identity. It's
a project I would shrink from, as I think most of us
would. For me, candidly, the difficulty of selecting
setting and icons (a dance studio? my office? books?
birds? champagne? the Oscar Mayer Wienermobile?)
is exacerbated by pride: being vulnerable to every
passerby's interpretations and judgments. I'm my
own example, a sensitive smart aleck who finds
Tony Harrell's odd stone charming . . . for a lard-
brick bureaucrat. We're all judged—by artifacts as
well as actions—but putting a whole life, pictorially,
on one hunk of rock takes a pharoah's assurance or
unselfconscious simplicity. I have neither.

Sports freaks have both—or their close cousins,
obsession and simplemindedness. Here comes a big
fat judgment. Fusing your identity to a football team
is sad. I don't mean indulging in a "rah, rah" now and
then. I mean putting a mascot on your tombstone.

To be fair, the fan in question had the Indian warrior-
mascot (with war paint) incised into a concrete graveside bench, not his headstone. Seven license plates
likewise celebrating the home team lean against the
stone. This man could be the self-styled "No. 1 Fan" of
our national-champions college team. Smiling, elderly,
resplendent in garnet and gold, concertizing on a
musical contraption combining drum, tambourine,
and what-all, No. 1 was a crowd-pleaser, win or lose.
As they say, football was his life. And his death.

Signed, Dated, and Planted

The Fan's first name was Lonnie, and he was a
"Jr." I wonder whether his father, on his stone, was
"Lonnie" as well. For someone who would have been

born around the turn of the century, the name Lonnie seems insufficiently old-fashioned. But there's no telling. One of my favorite old names in the cemetery is the flippant, flapperish Frosty McVay.

Ortencia, Alva, Carmelita: Were these old names the Jessicas, Jennifers, and Heathers of their day? A rash of Ortencia-namings is unlikely; perhaps the soft syllables came from a great-aunt or a grandmother. And if the young Ortencia Sophia Clayton (born 1894, died 1988) chafed under the weight of tradition, she no doubt took a nickname. Carmelita Reese did, and left it for us to ponder: "Butch."

A kindred spirit born in 1918, a "Beloved Mother," blasted off at eighty-two still known as "Dynamite." (She was, we also learn, "an inspiration to all who knew her." I'll bet.)

So it's not only odd stonework that piques my thoughts. I see that Maxie and Eva Johnson (husband and wife? sisters?) have their headstone in place, though neither is dead. That John and Ann Ferrero, "Loving Husband" and "Loving Wife," have thoughtfully spelled out what might be uncertain relations in their family plot. May Margaret Ferrero has the explanatory inscription, "John's mother"; Jim C. Poland (on the bride's side of the aisle) is "Ann's brother."

I see that most stones set down the very days of birth and death, though in various styles: the full and formal October 12, 1975; the abbreviated Jan. 5, 1922; the shorthand 2-1-97. Some emphasize the historical span: 1938-96. One wants the world to know *where*: "Died in Killarney, Ireland." Died there by design? By accident? Returned by air? By sea?

I see that monument carvers have seen (and

copied) it all: beat-up running shoes, new Nikes, electric guitar, skate board, a fishing rod (for him) and a tractor (for her).

I see that impermanent offerings, arrayed around the plots, last and last: shells, whirligigs, ceramic angels, plastic pelicans, valentine cookie cutters (hung from a tree).

I see that permanent inscriptions may be haunting in ways unforeseen. Some simple phrases, full and heartfelt, restore eloquence to cliche:

> *Always in our hearts.*
> *Joy Cometh in the Morning.*
> *Tomorrow holds no doubt for me.*
> *Nuestro Querido Amor.*

Some messages shift uncomfortably from the reassuring to the unsettling.

> *Stop dear children, as you go by*
> *As you are now, so once was I*
> *As I am now, you will be*
> *So dry your tears and follow me.*

Some epitaphs beg for deconstruction. One of Roselawn's most egomaniacal residents is the Rev. Althoff (b. 1879), who apparently had a transcriptionist in attendance as he transcended this shadowy life. On his substantial headstone, ALTHOFF thunders at us in six-inch letters, and on its back we read the

Exact words of
REV. C. B. ALTHOFF
JUST PRIOR TO HIS DEATH:

"A poor needy sinner died and received salvation most glorious.
While I lived, I tried to live a life of sacrifice for the service of others. I shall have the benefit of meeting him who gave his life for my salvation."

Now, I realize that Rev. Althoff is acknowledging his sin. (Sort of. He may or may not be the "needy sinner" himself.) I realize that he knows Jesus is Boss (though keeping Him unnamed). But this may be the most self-serving humility since Uriah Heep's. The Reverend is absolutely sure his salvation is sealed. Sacrifice plus service equals a glorious handshake at the pearly gates. The cost-benefit analysis clearly comes out in his favor.

I'm only mildly ashamed of my cynicism and sarcasm. The exact words are the reverend's. In his eighty-nine years, he no doubt helped hundreds and hundreds of people. Nothing undoes that good. But how many poor needy sinners leave granite advertisements for themselves?

I know. Judge not lest ye be judged. Of course you *are* judging me, so let me continue with some pure preferences. I don't like mausoleums. I like simple crosses. I find myself extremely drawn to the cemetery's few wooden cross—one seven feet tall—though I'm no longer drawn to the religion. I enjoy the flowered, planted graves, though I have neither the desire nor the thumb to create one.

The cemetery's most elaborately landscaped plot belongs to a teen-age boy, Beau. The phrase "working through your grief" is tangible here. Parents, friends, one person, many people . . . *someone* has created an Edenic bower for Beau's final sleep. The plot is huge, bordered all around with ornamental grass. It lies at Roselawn's southern edge, away from driving paths. Three unnecessary stone steps, allowed by the ground's slight swell, increase the grotto effect. Small Italian cypresses stand sentinel at two of the four corners. In another, a bench waits. In the last, chimes hang from a graceful pole, clinking over an oriental rock garden. An urn, a lantern, a candle, a small statue of St. Francis, shells, golf balls, stone tablets marked John 14:1–3, and two wrought iron chairs. It is lovely, sad, satisfying. And it will need tending for years to come.

Already Acquainted

If stones speak to us about the dead, if we read personalities from plots, it's only natural. We're mysteries all; and interpretations are ways of knowing. When I actually know the people resting in Roselawn, I'm confirmed that graves are clues and mirrors to the lives. A single six-foot plot always in bloom, carefully tended but not ostentatious, bears the name ESPOSITO—the family owning one of the city's best-known nurseries. An unusual alabaster monument, with slender columns supporting a lintel, graces the stone of NORA HURST—the wife of a celebrated local sculptor who personally chooses his stone in Italy.

Then I found the family compound of a neighbor. Mr. Fulghum was about eighty-six when I met him. I'd admired his home before without knowing who lived there. Vaguely Spanish in style, its prominent feature is a walled courtyard in which lush plantings are partially, enticingly visible. A rectangular flower garden in the front lawn changes regularly but always seems to be in bloom. It is a gardener's home.

One day a tall, vigorous, hatted, elderly man came walking into my yard, where I was raking pine straw, and offered me a cherry tree. Mr. Fulghum explained that he'd given cherry seedlings to everyone on the street—while my house was empty and for sale—did I want one? Assured I couldn't kill it, I accepted, and Mr. Fulghum went to get the tree and "his man," who did the digging. (Mr. Fulghum kept his vitality by knowing his octagenarian limitations.)

I got much more than a cherry. I got the story of Mr. Fulghum's life. He was a charming egoist, one of those people who simply assume the rest of the world is a waiting audience. Sometimes this relentless autobiography happens, or deepens, with age, though I suspect Mr. Fulghum bent ears even when young. But anyone with over eighty years behind him has, indeed, a great deal to tell, and I'm a sucker for it. He told about his cancer. He told about the many places he had worked. He told about hardships he'd overcome. He told about bringing the cherry seedlings from Virginia. I hardly remember the details. What I do remember is the romance of his marriage. He spoke about his wife, still, as his bride. They were married as teenagers, they were still together, and they were nearing a seventieth anniversary. He stood there, impressing me (as he knew he was) with his passion, unabashedly celebrating their intimacy with a stranger. Of all that he held forth about, love was the theme to which he vibrated. Old blowhard that he was, pausing in his narrative only to bark hole-digging orders at the black man he truly treated as property, Mr. Fulghum had not only known a grand passion, he had grown old with it, making it grander still.

The stories we tell of our lives are just that: stories. What we dramatize or minimize is always telling, and I knew Mr. Fulghum wasn't telling all. Still, what I found when I found his family in Roselawn, what I found he didn't tell me, was a shock. For a man obsessed with hardship and love, he never mentioned the buried babies. A son and twin daughters already lay underground, waiting for their elderly parents. A son who would have been more than sixty when I met his father.

I wasn't surprised at the careful, well-planted compound. He had bordered and divided the grave sites with timbers, just as he did the garden in his front yard. He had chosen glistening holly trees. And on the joint headstone for him and his bride, he had noted the date of their vows: "Wed Sept. 5, 1925."

Less than two years later, on February 1, 1927, James D. Fulghum, Jr., was born and died. What a bitter winter. Ten years passed. Christmas arrived. Again, Elizabeth's labor began. What pain, and joy, and pain. On December 26, Eva Jean and Ava Jane, "our darlings," were born. Ava, like her brother, has a single date on her stone. Eva lived for three days.

At first I wondered whether the Fulghums had chosen their house—which was built in the 1960s—to be near their children's graves. Then I realized that Roselawn didn't exist in 1927 or in 1938. No other graves are that old. The Fulghums brought their babies with them. Or at least their memories, rock-hard forever, a stone's throw away.

Mr. Fulghum is in the ground too now. His wife has left the house, and others tend the flowers and live behind the mysterious wall. I saw Mrs. Fulghum only once, at a neighborhood gathering. A tiny woman, she seemed almost feverishly gay. Later hints from my next door neighbor, a pastor's daughter, led me to suspect drink. I did go to the Fulghums' house once, collecting for the Leukemia Society, but friendly Mr. Fulghum did not invite me in. His wife's shadow flitted out of sight.

When did Mr. Fulghum's gardening begin? When did his wife begin to drink, if she did. What do you do when you're alone, all alone, with the love of your life?

Roselawn, for all its aspect of tranquil finality, is of course never at rest. It won't be, until every red-clay bed is turned down. I sometimes glimpse the bright blue undertakers' tents through my tall azalea hedge. I see them come and go as I walk, sprouting like brilliant mushrooms now here, now there, every few days or weeks. I see the massed flowers and temporary metal markers on dirt mounds; later, the unweathered stones. I study the new tributes to strangers, friends, and neighbors. I discover a name, a monument I've missed, unbelievably, before. Though it's not unbelievable. Years ago, at least four years, I found a headstone almost completely filled with the picture of a truck—and then I couldn't find it again. Did I hallucinate it? So struck was I by the unlikelihood of a Trailways bus and a large commercial truck parked in the same cemetery, I was *sure* it was there. Yet after fruitless looking—sometimes purposeful and sometimes in passing—I began to believe I'd dreamed it. Exactly two days ago, I found the phantom truck, not hidden at all, in plain view by a path.

A mystery solved. But always more loom. Till this moment, it never occurred to me that completely unmarked graves may hide in Roselawn. I see temporary markers that have become, by decades of default, a life's only monument. Why couldn't a marker rust away or be lost? Why couldn't an unmarked plot become completely grassed over, indistinguishable? My thoughts meandered here by looking out my office window, across the street, to Red Barber's house. Actually, his former house, where every Friday morning he broadcast his live, eccentric, fond conversation with Bob Edwards. His ashes are buried in the backyard, under his beloved camellias. They are his markers, his monument. ·

Red Barber died not long after Gary and I moved here, and we never knew him more intimately than as a cordial, hello-at-the-mailbox neighbor. I know better the retired couple who bought his house, put on the market because Lylah Barber could not live there, alone with her Alzheimer's. Living with and honoring the grave was a condition of the sale, though I don't think a legal one. My new neighbors feel honored themselves. How rare today to have a reminder of death so intimately near: part of your everyday life, touched and crossed by a family's coming and going.

In front of me, as I sit here, Red Barber rests unnamed, part of a suburban backyard garden. In back of me, beyond my own fenced yard, rest all the others: flamboyantly named, lovingly named, artistically named, guiltily named, temporarily named, unnamed. Whether shadowed by a massive stone or by a flowering branch, they are all, forever and ever, what one Roselawn monument so succinctly displays on its back—and what you and I are not:

STOCKSTILL

CHAPTER 2

The Plot Lengthens

I missed my brother's wedding, held in a cabin-sized, nineteenth-century chapel bordering Roselawn. I didn't his funeral, held in the large church next door. Eight years fell between; Gordon was thirty-three when he died. His wife, Liz, told me she went into the chapel, by herself, after the funeral and "lost it." I'm glad.

I picture her there, although—almost a decade and a half after Gordon's death and after years of living by the chapel—I've never been inside it. The taboo is odd even to me. Perhaps it's as simple as "thou shalt not trespass." But I wouldn't be. A historic marker invites visitors to Saint Clement's Episcopal Chapel, "built in Lloyd in 1890." Lloyd is an invisibly small rural community perhaps twenty minutes away. Why it was a site for a $3,500 church dedicated in 1895 by "Edwin Gardner Weed, third Bishop of Florida," and why the church was given an 1838 bishop's chair, "oldest in Florida," I don't know. The chapel was moved here in 1959 and rededicated by a fifth bishop. Containing "the original pine pews and reed organ," it is a wooden doll-house church fifteen by twenty-five feet, with pointed arches over the door and windows. All this I know from the outside.

Inside, just after Christmas 1975, my wonderful family gathered to marry Gordon and Liz, a happy, sudden event set after Gary and I had promised to go to California for the holidays. I was disappointed, but I didn't agonize. Gary's mother expected her grandchildren, and after all, we were lucky enough to live in the same town with Gordon and Liz. So I sat in a coffee shop in Santa Rosa, California, thinking of them, 3,000 miles away. Liz was beautiful. Gordon was beautiful. They were beaming. I've seen the photographs, which are the wedding to me.

Thus I saw the chapel for the first time only at his funeral, those eight years later. It wasn't the time for me to open the door and imagine the happiness I'd missed.

Wedding to funeral: the first circle of Roselawn in my life. The second: moving to the cemetery's edge, an almost equal number of years later.

Dramatis Personae

By that time, our family plot (Gordon's single-wide) was filling. We are, as mother once put it, "a cremation family" (a slightly scandalous condition to her Maryville, Tennessee, clan). Gordon's ashes were buried in a small wooden box—a fancy audiocassette holder, actually. When my father died and we wanted to bury his ashes here, Liz volunteered, "There's room in Gordon's plot. Of course we may not want to pile up too many more. It'll look like we're a bunch of short people."

See. Don't worry. I'm not planning to describe every heartbreaking detail of each terrible death. Our family is full of comic relief.

Though Gordon's stone was first, his death wasn't. Mother had died in Clearwater four years before. Perhaps the cast of characters, in and out of the plot, should be established. Hardly of Dickensian proportions, our six-member family was still larger than most of my childhood friends'. My mother and father, told at first that mother would never bear children, fertilely produced three girls before a boy: a decade's worth of birthing. The intervals got shorter as mother got older. Energetic, accomplished Andrea was first; my turn, four and a half years later; the golden-haired Gerber-baby Kerry, three and a half years; olive-skinned, velvet-skinned Gordon, a bit over two.

Only Kerry didn't marry. For balance, Andrea and I married twice each. By the time of Gordon and Liz's wedding, Gary and I had added our "blended" children to the family: my son, Lance; his daughter and son, Kristy and Ian.

Then in a single year in the late seventies, we heard, "It's cancer," three times. Twenty-six-year-old, athletic Gordon had the old man's disease, colon cancer. Mother arrived here for his surgery with a lump in her breast, about which she didn't speak, choosing to believe her doctors that it "was probably a cyst." It wasn't. When Gary's rare leukemia was diagnosed to round out the twelve months, Kerry, calling from Virginia, asked incredulously, "What's going on down there?"

A very good question. No doctor tried to answer it. In cancer's wrenching uncertainty, edicts are longed for but rarely given. Andrea's commentary was perhaps all that could be said: "It's spooky."

Gordon's surgery was successful; then we waited and watched. Gary's hairy-cell leukemia didn't even have a treatment; so we waited and watched. In Gordon's fifth healthy year, his doctor, who loved him, said, "You're cured. You are fine. Your cancer's gone. But I have to tell you: Your brother-in-law is not going to make it."

Two years later, Gordon was dead and Gary was cured. So much for edicts. Still, though, I'm glad Dr. McDonald told Gordon and Liz he was cured. I'm equally glad Liz didn't tell me Gary was doomed.

But back to the plot and mother's place in it. Her ashes aren't really at Roselawn, as your unreliable narrator said earlier. When more cancer was found two years after her surgery, it was already time for hospice. She wanted her ashes cast into the Gulf, which my father did alone. We had no ground for her—and didn't think of it as a lack, really. She was so present still. We all carried her. Today, though, since my father's death, her name is with his on the long, low, beautifully dark-marble "pillow" marker.

Two of her five brothers came from Tennessee for her funeral at Clearwater, probably not knowing there would be no graveside service. We walked into the church's community room for her memorial to find their huge horseshoe wreath, diagonally slashed with a ribbon tattooed "Mom." My uncles loved her, but did they think she'd entered Paradise or the Winner's Circle? Even if the florist's fault, that wreath is permanent family lore.

Not that the service was all reserved refinement. In swirled our parents' young Presbyterian minister, Bob Walkup, in a rainbow-hued, tie-dyed robe. What in the —? We found out. It was a moving tribute of goofy gravity. He stood before us in Jacob's many-colored coat a consummate visual rhetorician. He knew he looked exorbitant. He knew we were perplexed, expectant, nervous, a little pissed, all of the above. He didn't show he knew anything at all. He could have been in somber black and white.

Which is what he told us, as his eulogy progressed. He could have been traditional. For many people a rainbow robe would have been too much, too rich, too over-the-top for a funeral. But not for Myrtle. That was his refrain. But not for Myrtle. She was a well of surprising life to him, a woman who could have been his mother and whose thirsty mind pulled him along on her quest. She also liked a good joke. If you are a minister, what do you say about someone whose uniqueness and heart have marked you indelibly? What do you do? He didn't trust his eloquence alone. Or perhaps he did. Perhaps he had full confidence in his words to paint a person's life. But not for Myrtle.

Fools, Foils

If mother had that effect on her minister, you can imagine how she moved her first and, until months before her death, only grandson, Lance. He was thirteen when she died but seems in memory much younger. She was his first death, and he wouldn't let it in while she failed. Or he couldn't. He was quiet. There was puzzlement, simple incomprehensibility on his face. How could lively Nana change so and disappear? After her service, I saw him wandering on the ragged edge of the church property, picking up sticks fallen from the high pines. But when I called to him and went to meet him, he had only one stick, which he told me was to remember her, was to be her and that day. He looked at me then with no perplexity on his face, only loss, pure loss.

By the time of Gordon's death—Gordon who shared mother's gift of child-to-child play—Lance's look was distant and numb, though again he broke down finally at the service, by the grave, under pines at Roselawn. Only the family were at graveside, and as we walked back up the hill toward the church, seventeen-year-old Lance suddenly blubbered like a baby and couldn't walk. Someone whispered worry, but Liz briskly and compassionately showed the moment as it was: "Seems perfectly appropriate to me."

So we continued solemnly up the hill, our focal point—to the waiting mourners watching us—my stepson's newly mown, Mohawked skull. This was before shaved heads, spikes, and livid green locks jaded us all to weird head trips. When dad first saw Ian, he took me aside and whispered, "What happened to Ian's head?" Dad would have understood "lice" more easily than "bad timing."

Even Ian wished he'd delayed his fashion statement, as I knew when he had come to the dinner table, a few days before, with a blue work kerchief on his head.

Maybe he hoped I would assume "gypsy phase" and just dig into my dinner. He dreaded the unveiling. My face justified the dread. Rationally (and as a child of the Sixties) I knew it was just hair, or ex-hair; and I was too heart-sore to spend anger on teenage acting out; but I had to say, "I wish you'd waited." His face was remorse enough.

By the time of the funeral, we were used to Ian's strip-mined head. And it was a Gordon moment anyway: the ludicrous, the incongruous, the Three Stooges' mayhem in society settings. Six-foot-three Gordon was known to moo mournfully when caught in a herd of people exiting a lobby through one small door. Ian striding down the aisle with our decorous family—Mohawk not even slightly bowed, much less lowered in bovine submission—a Gordon moment, definitely.

Over the days from his death to his St. Patrick's Day wake and beyond, we veered from black grief to black humor. And no one veered more wildly than Liz. Crying in the chapel was private; giddy comedy was her public coping. On a particularly liquid family evening before the funeral, Liz decided to go along on a booze run to the liquor store. Since she was mid-martini, she took it along. Waltzing into the liquor store with her stemmed martini glass, Liz was queried about its contents. She stopped in her tracks. Heartbeat pause. "Would you believe water and an olive?"

Whatever Liz needed to do, no matter how wild, was fine with me. I had watched her. I had seen her with my brother. I knew her capacity for love. Of the abyss inside her now, I could only guess.

A lot of people loved Gordon, and even more admired him. I'm not elevating him to death's perfection. Gordon, especially in his wild drinking days, could tax Liz to the max. They also shamelessly popped off at each other when the family was together—and got over it almost as fast. Real people. That's it, perhaps. Gordon was extraordinarily real. He was physically beautiful too: tall, broad-shouldered, slim-waisted, high-boned. Sometimes covers do tell the book . . . *mine eyes dazzle; he died young.* Andrea, Kerry, and I taunted each other regularly about which one of us Gordon most "favored." Since he and I were the only olive-skinned, brown-eyed, dark-curly-haired ones, I clearly took the honor. Liz privately agreed. (Ha!)

Gordon's doctor, especially, knew him inside and out. Jack McDonald reacted to essence, not just presence. He saw the beauty, and he saw the disease. And he had helped the adoption happen—only two years after Gordon's diagnosis and surgery. Brendan came to Gordon and Liz as a fat, four-month-old cherub. Almost as soon as he arrived, his new Nana was dying. He had only a few months of her doting visits, and then he was the single squiggling, squirming outburst of life in her own home-turned-hospital.

So Brendan never really knew her, but then he didn't have to mourn her.

When his dad was lowered into Roselawn, Brendan was almost five. Mourning may be too sculptured an emotion for what he felt, but he felt. Brendan can't possibly remember Bob Walkup's rainbow robe, but he'll never forget Roselawn. It became his driving place. He and Liz would drive to visit the grave, and somehow they began a ritual of Brendan standing in Liz's lap, steering the car as they inched over the cemetery's untrafficked roads. I don't imagine it was calculated, but now Liz has given Brendan—car-crazy teen-ager Brendan—cemetery memories mixed of pleasure and pain.

Mixed blessings were all we had. Andrea found one, in the raw days after Gordon's death: "There was a good in mother's dying. She couldn't have stood this." Our dad didn't.

Diabola Ex Machina

Dad was already remarried when Gordon died, which meant he was already gone too. Oh, yes, there's a wicked stepmother in this tale. Purely evil, not one redeeming quality even admitting flawless skin, spun-silver hair, and the happiness she gave my father in the beginning.

He was as giddy as any new lover, and I was happy and relieved for him. He had found no other way out of his grief after mother died—not visits to children, not tennis, not drinking. When mother's surgeon had come into the waiting room to say, "Inoperable," my father burst out, "I can't imagine living without her." That was his truth, the radicalness of their union and of his unmooring. Perhaps in some ways all grief is a failure of imagination. To end it, the unimaginable has to happen. Rebecca was it.

Even before we met her, and when all of us were unanimously happy dad had found her, his phone calls moved from delight to tearful accounts of her "hard life" and fears of our resentment. Alarms should have sounded. After Rebecca's initial outpouring of charm, during which she actually got her ring and her marriage, Andrea, Kerry, and I took turns being her villains. (Never Gordon, who in fact disliked her at once.) Continually, she felt slights so unspeakable she couldn't speak them even to dad, who remained puzzled but dutiful to the end. She separated dad from his friends and from his sister. She dictated letters chastising his beloved grandson, Lance, for an awkward greeting on the phone. She quit her job (because her boss persecuted her). She got a stake for her daughter's jewelry business and a home near the beach (all of which we thought fine, not knowing our father's finances). She convinced dad that a sign of "No Visitors" on Gordon's hospital room meant him and yanked him huffily back to Clearwater.

By the time for Gordon's funeral at Roselawn, we were all so exhausted, torn, and angry that I did not meet my father and his wife at the airport. I asked a family friend. Since she had by then defined us all as bitches, why not enjoy the persona? The friend knew dad well but Rebecca not at all, so I explained cattily, "He'll be with a woman in purple." In fact, Rebecca overcame her color fetish to wear black, but the purple prose flowed in a recriminative letter after they returned to Clearwater. Everyone played nice at the funeral, and for my father it wasn't playing. He loved us too much and for too long, and he hurt too deeply.

But out of our presence, Rebecca reigned supreme. My airport slight was the only real one out of the dozens she fabricated, but even in Gordon's memory, or because of it, I couldn't apologize. To dad's (ghostwritten) letter bewailing our sin, I wrote my one intemperate, hurtful letter to him. They're both in the Dad File, an epistolary chronicle of two final failures—not imagination—that I had to face: words and will. I believed that if I, if anyone, loved powerfully enough and could express that love and its rightness lucidly, forcefully, eloquently . . . Adverbs were not enough.

With every strained encounter, new accusation, or unsatisfactory conversation, I wrote. Before the funeral. After the funeral. I did apologize. I analyzed. I pleaded. I said we must not let this happen every way I knew how. And I missed him.

Finally, he wouldn't see his daughters any more and told me by mail that all communication would cease because . . . because . . . because we just weren't doing right. That's the gist, whatever the letter said. He didn't really write it. It was too graceless. I didn't spend an overabundance of years in graduate-school "close reading" not to know my father's masculine, masterful prose style.

Then it hit me: He doesn't have to answer. I can't hope for correspondence, but I can write into the void. I wanted him to know, because I knew he still cared. What his grandson was doing; what kind of young man he was becoming; both the momentous and the mundane of our lives. I was so pleased with this solution, and so naive. Words, will, acts. I thought death their only defeator. Rebecca shoved my face hard into the world. His pen pushed by her evil spirit, dad wrote back to say, *Don't think we don't know what you're doing. You won't give up, will you? We can have no communication.* So, yes, I could write out my soul, but there was no point in sending it. I mailed one last Father's Day card. Andrea and Kerry didn't.

My sisters and Gordon all saw dad's weakness and complicity. They were right. Rebecca's twisted whisperings didn't alone keep him away. He couldn't stand watching his only son die. Then he couldn't stand watching his oldest daughter disintegrate when her marriage ended. He couldn't and wouldn't take it. He had rationales for withdrawing from them: *I know Gordon wants this last time with his wife and child. I'll respect his privacy. I love Andrea and would never get involved in troubles between a man and wife.*

But there's the rub: the misguided, misapplied, blinkered code of conjugal loyalty that our father lived by. He wasn't only weak. The sacred marriage vow was no cliché to him. His fidelity was absolute. He had lived it when it wasn't easy, through mother's alcoholism and recovery. But he had lived it then with someone worth it: with a flawed woman so good at heart, so strong, and so in love with him that being fused to her indeed created a new, better being for them both.

Ah, but if you marry a succubus. Then does his Scottish fealty become a tragic flaw? Or the shameful cloak of a cowardly man? Either, both, it was his undoing.

Interlude

Bring in the clowns. Please. We seem to have stumbled into one of Poe's accidental sarcophagi. *Help, you expire.* Those headstones had their moments. Now we're exploring the terrain six feet under and the oxygen's fading fast.

Okay. I'm remembering chocolate milk. A tea party with chocolate milk. Andrea and her friend (and I) have on dresses. The ice-cream parlor table and chairs, child-sized, are set up on the lawn. It is Andrea's day, her guest. She is excited. I am tolerated. I am jealous.

I am also totally silent, and no one sees it coming. Not even I.

Miss Priss sits on her chair. I have a very full, not doll-sized, cup of chocolate milk. I am watching the cruelly preening girl from a distance, from somewhere outside the charmed circle of the table. Jump cut. I am directly behind the still smiling, unsuspecting guest, with my party cup raised, and then chocolate elixir is cascading onto the very center of her head, over her face, over her dress, oh verily I hope into her shoes.

The world stands still. She is so dumbfounded she does not move or cry out. And when she does, I do not hear it. I remember almost nothing beyond that moment. There must have been screams, shouts, mother, punishment. All lost! What I do have, though, is so pure. No catharsis before or since more satisfying. The instant itself. I was doing wrong, I was doing right. I chose, I did not choose. The moment of milk hitting head was absolute, complete relief and revenge. It was a full and finished act, no matter how naughty: sweet, sticky, and just deserts.

The Smoking Gun

Well, enough of this hilarity.

We are coming back to Roselawn, but it will take a few phone calls.

One (in). Lance, passing in the hallway, is stopped dead when I answer and exclaim, "Dad!" I cannot express how happy his far-away voice makes me. Even my father's unhappiness bodes joy, because the breach has come. The communication: *I know one thing. My marriage is over. She has nothing to do with me. I have no friends. No, we aren't living apart. I can't support one household. No, this doesn't mean you can call now; it just inflames her. I got the Father's Day card.*

No real response when I say that that he can be with me, that we all want him. Agreement when I say that she is sick and mad. No real committal when I ask for a promise that he will call again—but no denial either.

Two (out). Andrea, Kerry, and I in conference call. The communication: *This is it. This is different. This is a beginning. We must get to him and get him away. I'll go. In person, he'll see that he isn't trapped. It's not a defeat to come to his children.*

Three (in). My advance scout in Clearwater calls a few days later, the same friend who brought dad and Rebecca from the airport to Gordon's funeral. The communication: *Ellen, I think you need to get down here now. Something is wrong. Mr. Abernethy killed himself.* I am on the floor of my office. The receiver is ricocheting from desk to chair to Gary's hand—he says words and hangs it up. I have never before lost consciousness while awake. I have never been standing and then screaming on the floor with only a black hole in between.

Four (out). Not long after. Amazingly, not long after. I am steely, which is probably why neither Gary nor Lance tries to stop me. They sit on the couch, an unseen, perfectly still audience, while I dial Rebecca from the oracle of death in my office. She answers with a perfect tremulousness in her voice; no doubt others are with her too. She has been comforted, petted, solaced in her aggrieved shock. She expects more. The communication: *Dad called me three days ago, Rebecca.* Suddenly stiff silence. She did not know. *He told me his marriage to you was over. He told me about your cruelty. He knew that you are insane. I want you to know that I*

know you killed my father.
It wasn't chocolate milk, but it was close.

Unraveling

Liz intervened to get the ashes. She took Rebecca's abuse for my reckless truthtelling and took it gladly, because we knew he could not rest with anyone but us. So the plot accepted him. One breathless summer day Kerry, Andrea, Liz, Gary, and I circled Gordon's ground again. My best friend Martha unexpectedly joined the circle, shy in a filmy sundress. Martha still had a father, but I don't think she ever had much of him. One evening long before, Martha happened to visit Gary and me when mother and dad were there. We were all standing in the living room. Dad and I kissed each other on the lips; I don't remember why. And I saw Martha's face, watching us. So much played there that I'll never know. Here she was.

No one has ever asked me how my father died. He was seventy-three. They didn't know his vigor. I want to say a broken heart. It's as true as a bullet.

Many times man lives and dies
Between his two eternities, ...
Whether man die in his bed
Or the rifle knocks him dead,
A brief parting from those dear
Is the worst man has to fear.
Though grave-diggers' toil is long,
Sharp their spades, their muscles strong,
They but thrust their buried men
Back in the human mind again.

I chose the poem. Andrea read it. Mother and dad's marker is very fine. Liz and I chose the raw rock at the stoneworks where she found Gordon's. It is uniquely beautiful to me—and characteristically wrong. I couldn't remember the date of mother's death. The day, yes, not the date. Kerry knew it instantly when I asked. Andrea instantly knew it was wrong when she saw the carved stone. At last a solid memorial for our mother, a chiseled tribute for ashes that long ago suffered a sea change—and her own daughters can't get it right. What an outrage! But not for Myrtle. For Myrtle: two names, one stone, all right.

When my father called me, he said something else: *Just tell me one thing, Ellen. We were a happy family once, weren't we?* Only delirious hope for more happiness, happiness restored, could have so blinded me to that good-bye. The answer was and is yes, yes, and yes. Happy families, all alike, don't make good stories. Their pain, all different, can.

CHAPTER 3

Transients

I walk onto the verge of the dead through a chain-link gate, by the woodpile, in the far corner of my back yard. The gate swings open on a tall tangle of azaleas, so that I must turn right on a narrow path (behind my neighbor Allie's manicured yard-park) to reach the verge's pine-dotted expanse. When Gary and I moved in, I thought the path was Allie's. Since she has no back fence or hedge, Allielawn and Roselawn have a vague demarcation. I told her I hoped she wouldn't mind my swerving a few feet onto her domain. She was gracious—not enlightening me that it was city property anyway.

Possessiveness is easy to understand, though Allie's and mine are different. I like to be in the cemetery, she to incorporate it. The more I walked, the more at home I became, the more I saw. Graveyards are worlds of the living too, though we breathing ones evacuate overnight. Like a runner who pounds the same path through a neighborhood every day, or a couple who sit on their brownstone stoop every evening, I am a witness simply by being there. People come and go, never talking of Michelangelo.

Well, they might. Barb and I talk nonstop on our weekly walk together. Usually we converse, or at least share time. Occasionally, though, one or the other of us holds forth for the whole stint, unloading frustration about family, work, children, poodles (Barb and Mark's children), and various villains thwarting our peace of mind. The pace picks up on these days. It doesn't need saying that the receiving party has her day on a future walk.

Treks with Barb are a combination of exercise, friendship, and stress release; we're more fixed on each other than on our surroundings. My walks alone are more open to the world, though the calculated intent is, by being out in the world, in motion, to clarify my inner world. Smashing writer's block: a less lofty way of putting it. And God knows, most of what I write isn't lofty. But whether I'm writing ad copy for Panhandle Pets, or trying to conceive a new campaign for a bank, or stuck inside a paragraph about time in the Renaissance (for a textbook), putting one foot in front of the other usually kicks the block over.

In my experience, any kind of writing, while always requiring concentrated butt-in-the-chair effort, must have its sideways side. You can sit in front of your piece of paper or stare straight into your computer screen, but it's in the walk to the refrigerator, or on the drive back from the meeting, or in the stroll around the cemetery, that the word or idea flies right into your temple—somewhere behind the eye, present only in peripheral vision, a brain gift. The how-to article I'll never write for aspiring authors is called "In Praise of Piddling, Fiddling, and Fooling Around."

So sometimes I'm in the cemetery with a notebook and pen, walking, stopping, and scribbling. Only once has someone asked me what I was writing (after all, it could be love letters or hate mail). The male part of a sixtyish, charming-looking couple bolted away from the female part and blurted, "I can't help it. I said to my wife, I'm going to ask what she's writing, and she said, you won't do that, and I said, she won't mind, I'm just curious." So there. For his romantic and friendly sake, I was really sorry that it was a pet food day, not a Renaissance Time day.

I don't see that couple any more. Maybe they've moved on, joining the ranks of Roselawn tourists, the ones who do one-time mourning business and don't linger, or the ones who try it out as 'greenspace' but don't succumb to its charms. Roselawn is not a busy place. Cars and mourners of course come through daily, though only in ones or twos (except for buryings). Even when I don't see visitors, I see their leavings: the fresh gift, from lilies to jack-o-lanterns to birthday balloons.

Occasionally I see a runner, even more seldom skate boarders. There's a group of four or so skateboarders in the neighborhood, incredibly lanky boys in even lankier pants. They're sweet. I've decided they are because they once actually spoke to the middle-aged woman they keep encountering in the streets. They do look innocent somehow: not threatening, not tough; secretive, yes, but then what else can teens be, secrets even to themselves? I get the impression that their skateboard time in the neighborhood is just noodling. We have nice long hills, they're usually packing their boards, why not use them when they're hanging? Serious skating, I think, goes on elsewhere. But not in Roselawn. I wondered at first why they weren't there. Now if I were a skateboarder . . . Then I considered the restraints of society, setting, and law. Even semi-rebellious boys might have principled feelings about whizzing past people trying to get their eternal rest.

Downstairs, Upstairs

The real regulars of the cemetery—besides the sleepers, me, the smiling Scottie-dog man, and the I'll-speak-but-I'll-never-smile! man—are Mr. Britt and his crew. It's good the skaters don't covet Roselawn's gentle hills. Mr. Britt is so easygoing and kindly that I imagine he would regret kicking them out. He's not there daily, having other cemeteries to oversee, but usually some of his men are: mowing, edging, digging, sodding fresh mounds, moving dead plants and weathered plastic pots to the car paths for pick-up. Their base of operations is the four-square, cement-block work shed on Roselawn's south side (near Beau's grotto). Oak-sheltered, it reticently commands the graveyard's last frontier, the last sweep of open, unplotted slope.

Still a young man, sandy-haired Mr. Britt cruises in and out of the cemetery in a city truck, elbow out the window, as I imagine he does in his own truck on the weekends. I got to know him by name and in person through Allie, or through her paranoia. One day Gary looked down our backyard and saw new daylight. The tall azaleas were whacked; Roselawn's gravestones were in view. Uh oh: Round 2 with Allie. Gary and she had already sparred, with a split decision, over the street light she erected in her back park. After our previous house, hemmed-in among neighbors on a busy corner, Gary had truly lusted after a private back yard, a place to sit unseen, restfully, in daylight or dark.

Allie—a retired, never-married home economics professor (setting an ambiguous educational example) —not only installed a huge light on a twenty-foot pole, but the light buzzed. Loudly. While I noticed the sound effects only after Gary pointed them out (his musician's ear), I heard what he meant. I wouldn't, though, have done what he did: have a face-to-face (his psychologist's soul). I didn't care about the light and sound because our large garage and its driveway buffeted them, but he did. I also avoid confrontations— a reason I'm not in a 'helping profession.' So Gary, obsessing in his mild-mannered bulldog way about the eye and ear affront, made his neighborly visitation alone.

Allie couldn't believe it. Especially from a new neighbor who let all the leaves fall before raking a single one. You see how the dialogue degenerated. Gary managed to pull the session to a calm close, but Allie's only clear concession was to take care of the buzzing. She would "look into" a shield over our side of the light. She wouldn't hear of taking the light down. Not with all the menaces she imagined sneaking through her yard from the dark wilds of the cemetery.

Allie was an original resident of the subdivision; she'd directed the building of her house, as she proudly pointed out. Now retired, she had more than a little sense of herself as feudal lady of Piedmont Park village. She bristled at any criticism of her manor. But she raised a huge stink about another neighbor's "illegal" children's playhouse. And she told Mr. Britt to whack those menace-harboring azaleas.

So we met our cemetery's caretaker. Mr. Britt wanted only to accommodate. Our neighbor wanted her sight-lines clear and her azalea hedges tidy. Now knowing we didn't, he would leave our privacy screen to grow and grow and grow, which it has. He even endorsed my lazy method of removing the aforementioned offending leaves: dump 'em on the azaleas as mulch. Mr. Britt recognized Roselawn's status as a special domain with shadowy borders, and through his eyes I saw it from the inside-out too. He tended a city within a city, with responsibilities to the dead, their living, and the quick on its perimeter.

It is constant, of course, the men's cycle of mowing, edging, wreath removal. Even fabric flowers fade, wilt, drop petals, and scatter on the wind. City road crews also come. They would probably like to come more often, to spread hot tar where no hurried drivers whiz past, where shade trees are steps away, where no white lines are needed. Where they can chat with people. The black-haired, toothy boy I talked with certainly seemed to be enjoying his gig. Admitting that a lot of city streets needed his ministrations more than Roselawn, he grinned, "I dunno how they decide. We got the order, here we are." Then heartily: "Won't be more'n a few days. We'll leave you in peace!"

They left me a present more sure: a few delicate dogwood branches, twigs really, fallen and pressed into the tar's wet surface. The twigs have moldered, but their ghosts remain in the hard, dry road: feathery intaglio branchings beneath my feet.

Alone Together

Maybe I'm beginning to look like a cemetery ghost myself. Not a spook, but a haunter. Mr. Britt remarked on it, "I noticed you walk a lot. Wear a hat, don't you?" My walking clothes no doubt gave me away to the road worker too. And to the stranger who sobbed out about her mother's flowers? I'm not sure. I was startled but not wary, only sorry in my uselessness. Her arms full of partly wilted blossoms, all her grief wrapped in indignation, she didn't plan to speak to me. She couldn't help herself. Behind her, a hundred feet away at their mother's new grave, her sister stood, wrapped in herself. She would not gush. I could have guessed they were sisters, both honey blond, plump, still dressed in their office clothes.

"They took her flowers! Our mother." She choked. "Someone just took them off the grave and dumped them here. Who would do such a thing?" The cemetery workers I explained, feebly. Usually they were not so zealous. She took a shaky breath and turned to return all she now had to give her mother. She had no more to say, or she had so much more. Briefly, I wished I'd said more, maybe something would have comforted — perhaps that the workers' intent was respectful. They watched for toppling, withering wreaths; who knew when mourners would come back to prune brown blooms?

But her question was mostly statement. She may have forgiven the workers later. She may have been doing it as she turned away. Her wet eyes did not look as wild to me. Her anger was out. She had a task, and a waiting sister.

I was headed home that day, nearing the work shed. The road follows the open grassy hill that drops down to Roselawn's lowest point, where in fall and winter days you actually feel the temperature fall as you descend. It's a pocket of cool. The slope in sunlight almost always makes me smile. It's an emerald trigger for my childhood; it's any smooth and grass-scratchy meadow at whose height I would lie down sideways, arms straight at my sides, and roll giddily down. I see us—who were we? cousins? friends?—scattered all over a hill, tumbling down at different speeds, some sprawled midway, some safe and exhilarated at the bottom. At the bottom of Roselawn's rolling hill is a person-high pile of red clay and a cross-section of a big oak, lying there not on its stump end, but on its side. A roller could miss them, though.

One day I approached the felled trunk from the other side, as I was starting my walk. I wasn't descending the hill but approaching it. Then I saw them and stopped. Two little girls, blond again, sat on the log, their backs to me. They sat so close their thin shoulders touched. Sometimes a head would turn in profile to the other, gently. I was too far away to hear whether they were talking, but even if they were, conversation wasn't the aim. They were too lazy, too still. I was rooted and couldn't help myself, didn't want to. Such peace: I wanted to savor it. In a sentimental painting, their arms would have encircled each other's waist.

I was sentimental enough without this touch. I've fixed them forever in my memory painting. I don't even remember moving from my trance. I don't remember turning, to leave them to their peace; or going on toward them, to put myself into their solitude and alter all. I only remember looking; seeing their fine, stringy hair on their shoulders, their slightness, their delicate profiles, their total intimacy, their private play world, their quiet, their childhood.

Fugitive Souls

Their beer-drinking future selves favor a spot just a little beyond: a concrete culvert, graffiti-sprayed, that interrupts an odd berm on this southern boundary of the cemetery. Walking along the narrow high bunker, I'm up above long back yards of distant neighbors. No fences or azalea hedges could keep out prying eyes, but impenetrable kudzu does. Those on this side of Roselawn have something better than azaleas. They have a jungle wall of green, its growth so fast it's visible. The culvert is meant for runoff, though it never looks wet, just damp. I skirt it because it makes a deep step down, but its depth has to be its sole inviting quality to reckless youth. It's a hidey hole. Hiding the occasional beer can. I've seen kids around the berm even in the daytime, their sporty trucks parked below. They cast furtive glances at me, like adolescent spies caught in a clandestine contact. It's unrealistic to think teen-agers won't seek out a cemetery. At night, walking with friends, I've seen them parked or cruising through. And sometimes in the big back bedroom, with its wall of sliding glass doors, I catch the glint of leaf-filtered headlights. But suburban Roselawn, luckily, isn't a regular hangout. Drunken shouts and racing motors are rare.

And how do I know all of Roselawn's cans and bottles are theirs? I don't. The empties don't belong to the residents, living or dead, but they could have other importers, as I found. My explorations of our new neighborhood took a while. The streets wind and loop, unlike the short, neater blocks of our old, more citified neighborhood. Whether heading out my front door toward the duck pond down the hill, or crossing the cemetery and emerging from its other side, I found myself daunted by the long blocks and large lots, by the confusing turns, by the necessity either to retrace my steps or take a slow spiral home. I got lost. And I got over it. Unless I wanted Roselawn to become my own endless loop, more picturesque than the Geezer Parade's but equally closed, I had to let curiosity blunder on through the maze.

One day, on a rambling walk beyond the cemetery, I found myself at an unexpected dead end. Ahead wasn't just woods, but woods with an entrance, and a path, and a boardwalk over a creek, and a bench. It was dark, secret, and odd. A find. I was back to the Nancy Drew-obsessed girl who biked side roads hoping for mysterious retreats and turning solitary houses into spooky ones. The oddest thing about Brinkley Glenn, as I discovered it was named, was its narrowness. I had no idea where I was that first day. Trees form for most of the park's length a total canopy; entering in its middle, I couldn't orient by sight.

One main path offered itself. Tentative, overgrown branchings off of it might or might not be trails. I tried one, which petered out into brambled undercover. I tried another, which brought me a few scratches later to traffic noises. Three steps up a sandy bank and I knew where I was. Cars whizzed by on four-lane Meridian Road, the suburb's western perimeter. I wasn't in the wilderness. I was in a strip-oasis between comfortable "Waverly Hills" houses and the thoroughfare that took their owners to the mall. Brinkley Glenn was Brinkley's (or someone's) quixotic gift to the city elders. "So what if it's two blocks long and only a deep lot wide: Do you want it for a city park or not?"

They did. Walking the main path to its southern end, you find the unassuming entrance—actually between houses—with its carved wooden sign. It's right on the corner of Waverly Road, just before the stop sign at Meridian. I'd driven by it hundreds of times. Driving blind.

I wondered who knew about it, who used it, who took refuge there. Teen-agers, again. They're the only other people I've encountered, though surely the homeowners on the strip's edge must seek out its cool shade now and then. It's also a great place for birding, especially of winter migrants. The weather was turning cool when I found the Glenn (so named to fit the neighborhood's Sir Walter Scott identity; never mind that the glen's sluggish stream is storm drainage). On a second trip, I followed another faint path, still believing one might lead somewhere. It did. I walked into a hobo camp—and right back out. "Homeless" is the word now. No one was home at the moment, no one to sense my startled chill at seeing the huge drum stove. I had the eerie sense of a trespasser on the trespassers' domain, an outsider without an outsider's I.D. Fear is probably inappropriate, but there it was, even if faint. Whoever slept here wasn't lying low in a brigands' encampment, biding time for forays into the wealthy's manors. They just wanted to be warm, and hidden. This skinny remnant of a forest served them much better than a big city park, with driving roads that police could patrol after the posted sundown closing. What was remarkable was that the homeless were so few feet from the park's path and yet so successfully leaf-curtained off. Nancy Drew they didn't expect.

Of course, they should have. The nosey smarty was always getting trapped in thieves' hideouts, so that her readers' pulses could pick up as she got tied up. Later, I returned to Brinkley Glenn, though I didn't stray again from the path until months later. It was murderously hot that day. No big fires were needed. But the whole drum was gone—as it should be. Little girls and boys of Waverley Hills didn't need homeless, perhaps not wholly harmless, hidden in their park, drinking wine by firelight. Yet I hadn't turned them in. And they didn't just move on. They were found out and turned out. "The park closes at sundown."

So, yes, Roselawn's occasional empty pint may be a hobo's, not a high schooler's. No camp will appear, though. Hardly a bed roll could be hidden, much less a 55-gallon drum. Bigger than Brinkley Glenn, Roselawn nevertheless is not hospitable to living lodgers. A headstone may make a nice backrest for unbathed brothers sharing a bottle, but this city property is a retreat of last resort. Too much traffic, even if the nights are dead quiet.

Exits, Entrances

"Are you walking out here all by yourself?" She knew perfectly well I was, unless I had my imaginary friend along. "Ooh, you should be careful, you know." It's true that I was skirting the west edge of Roselawn, which becomes a brambly band of trees—the cemetery's one fully blind and impassable border. But it's not that blind, the day was full, and the woman herself was quite alone, tending a grave. She wanted to talk. Or rather, to show and tell.

"Will you look at how these flowers have lasted? It's been days, but see—lots are fine. Isn't that something?" The grave was fresh, and on it were huge sprays of flowers. I remember yellow glads, which were lovely. Maybe flowers resting on the clay last longer than wreaths, windblown on their tripod stands. She was truly pleased. I was suitably admiring.

It was her son-in-law's grave. And there was her late husband's. And there would be hers. Her space had, in fact, had a little premature practice.

"I came out here, and they'd dug up my plot for my son-in-law." She tossed this off as one of those blunders to be put up with from workers ("Had to fill it back in, of course.") and kept right on going with the tour. Yes, the mess and confusion put her out. Me, it jolted—though I had to wait for my emotions to register. We were moving on.

Here, I did have time to think, was a real cemetery haunter: one of those people, women often, who tend a family plot as if it's another room in the house—sort of an off-premises addition that has to be kept tidied for visitors and general cosmic order. This was not a doom-and-gloom pilgrimage.

Perhaps in her late sixties, perhaps more, Mrs. Bryant was steel gray and spry. The relish of her supposedly dismal duties could have repelled me, but she was just too personable. What if she was family plot–fixated, if she showed off dying funeral bouquets as though they were prize pansy beds? She might be living her life in a cemetery, but she wasn't having any part of the Long Black Veil.

Then suddenly she announced, pointing diagonally off toward another grouping of stones, nicely hedged, "My husband's plot is in that pretty one over there. He'll be close by, with his wife." I wasn't confused for long. Held there between her two domains, I saw the light as this female Mr. Fulghum held forth. Oh, she had lost a husband; but she had also gained another piece of Roselawn.

"Met him right here. My daughter and I came to tend my husband's grave, and there he was, at his wife's." She didn't volunteer who opened the conversation. Given her forwardness with me and his apparent carpe diem spirit, I would flip a coin rather than guess. "He started calling me right away. Just immediately. Couldn't put him off." By now she was back in the pleasure of the memory, sharing a smile more secret than boastful: "I married him six months later." Her story was told. She released me easily with a cheery, "Nice talkin' —might see you again."

Do lovers who meet in cemeteries ever think of marrying there? Probably not. In bowling alleys, yes; underwater in scuba tanks, yes. Yet I now knew one reason my friendly accoster looked on the graveyard as homely ground, a place of ordinary life, not just death. Her life, and the widower's, took new life there. It is a piece of my piecing of Roselawn that I relish. I do think still of the eerie moment when an aging woman went to check on the digging of a younger man's grave and found her own, gaping at her feet. It would unsettle me, that bureaucratic error. It did. Yet

Mrs. Bryant had learned that life's holes can be filled as unexpectedly as they appear, even right where she stood. As long as the living set their feet on the same ground in which others molder, a cemetery cannot be wholly a place of death.

People come and go, and work and cry, and meet and wed.

My house is on the east side of Roselawn, which means that I watch the light of the setting sun bathe its entire expanse. One near-twilight I began a walk. Hurricane Gordon was besieging Florida. No threat to Tallahassee, that evening he still showed us his colors, a lurid queer light nevertheless golden. Dusk was so close that every object, tree or stone, was either a dark thickening or a radiant glowing.

I was not alone in this otherworld, I found. To my left—very near the cool dip, the girls' stump, the spies' hiding—I saw that a blanket was spread on the grass near a grave. It was an impossibly dark-golden tableau. A woman stood at the fabric's edge. Another young one, deeply brunette, sat on the blanket. Both were lost, as was I, in what also lay there: a baby, as plump as any Renaissance cherub. The scene could have been an idyllic picnic. But it wasn't. It offered up a fragile delicacy far better: a luminous, heartbreaking, oblivious new being, bathed in a dying light.

CHAPTER 4

Clean White Angels

The voices of Roselawn are children's. Squeals and laughter. So familiar were the bubbling shouts that at first they didn't register. Besides sirens and traffic, the ambient noise at our old house included rowdy recess at the day care catercornered across Sixth Avenue. After a zoning change, a home very like ours suddenly sprouted children, playing happily in a sand yard behind a high wire fence. The little yahoos ran about breathing carbon monoxide just feet from whizzing cars. As a former day care mom, I thought about this hazard, but I enjoyed the cheery racket. Healthy lungs, anyway.

That's why the voices drifting out from the Episcopal day school seemed so natural. The children's extensive play area (also sanded) is at the back of the church buildings, elevated over a corner of Roselawn. Standing in the cemetery, you look up through unkempt bushes, gnarled roots, and chain link, the children's feet at your head. Walking there only recently with Andrea, Liz, and her youngest son, Logan (her second child-blessing since her remarriage), I'd forgotten it was Sunday, church time. We came abreast of the nursery area just as children spilled out like hyped-up monkeys at the zoo, racing everywhere—and then spotting us. The brashest, most curious hit the fence, imps clinging like chimps, and turned the tables on the zoo metaphor, as monkeys will. Maybe they were inside the fence, but we were the ones on view.

"Hey!" cried a deep-voiced little tank of a boy. "Who are you?" Logan, ordinarily a big "Hey!" man himself, definitely felt on the wrong side of the wire, slinking along with three Big People instead of chasing through the play-gazebo, tantalizingly decorated with gingerbread men. If wishes were ponies, Logan would have been long-gone. The children's several taunting questions not receiving satisfactory replies (Liz pleasantly asked, "And who are you?"), the lead imp finally blasted out, "Whatcha doin? Walkin in the graveyard?"

Having sized up the situation as nothing more interesting than that, he and his followers swung back to the jungle gym. I had been walking in the graveyard for weeks before I found its other children.

Abbreviated

It's at the west end of the cemetery, on a ragged edge, like the nursery. I was making a big, off-road circuit that day, walking the largest possible circumference instead of following the car paths. Apparently I'd finished rummaging through my own head, because I was reading stones, eyes traveling the ground. Baby Girl Leckinger, Jan. 1, 1962. Eric Todd Anderson, 5/18/68. Baby Boy White. Odd, I thought, these graves so close together, until a chill of recognition swept in, stopped me cold, and unbowed my head. Not three, but dozens of miniature markers spread out before me. I was in the children's corner.

Infants' graves punctuate Roselawn. I had seen not only the Fulghums' transplanted twins but the graves of other children—one the son of an elderly neighbor from Sixth Avenue. I couldn't mistake his name, Zach Shelley, on the stone; this long-buried child had to be his. Yet as disquieting as every noticed newborn was, an entire congregation of tiny plots was a deep disturbance. Or perhaps not congregation but segregation, setting apart, difference, anomaly, all wrong and all together.

The scale, the accumulation, the anonymous inscriptions both flat and wrenching: these stones chilled. The unnamed are the oddest, though I know well it's not so odd. Lance was born without his name chosen. Even today, with sonograms and amniocentesis, parents may remain indecisive until the babe itself demands identity; in the past, birth was fundamentally uncertain. Boy or girl, blue or pink?

Thus Infant Girl Chittum. And INF SON of Mr & Mrs Robert B. Futch. And The eternal daughter of Robert L. and Ellen L. K. Knight. Even with the child named, on these small markers the mothers and fathers loom large. Their identity, too, their future, is now diminished — a loss told on diminutive headstones that cheat even words of their letters.

MELISSA E. HARRELL
INFANT DAU. OF
CHARLES & PATSY M.
AUG 18, 1968

More sorrowful still is the air of abandonment, of neglect — rare in Roselawn. Toppled toys have never been righted. Ancient plastic bouquets, sun-bleached to dirty paleness, lean askew on headstones. Don't the workers tend here? Heavy equipment is in fact often parked off the skinny sward at this edge of the cemetery, pulled onto an almost hidden clay road that quickly goes nowhere — for this is the blind, brambly, Mrs. Bryant district. It could be a fine and private place, as evidently someone else once thought. A half-collapsed wooden picnic table now invites neither workers nor families nor me. Rusty machinery, rotted wood; this is the far reach of Roselawn.

Pacing the whole children's area recently, I realized it seemed an abandoned cemetery (a phrase we take for granted but which suggests so much about the dependencies of the living and the dead. When, why, and how do we abandon those who have so decidedly abandoned us?). Only two days later I returned and felt something was different. Had those chrysanthemums, bright plastic bunny sunglasses, and motorcycles rested at the foot of Kevin Caldwell Simmons' stone? They had not. I knew it certainly when I saw the plastic milk jug (for watering) hiding behind the stone: modernly fat-free. This child was lost six years ago, a new toddler of one year and one month, but someone still bought and brought him toys. Moving on a few rows, I saw that someone else had visited to plant mums and coleus on a grave almost fifteen years older—for a boy, Justin, whose one day of life had now been mourned for eighteen years.

Hastened

From where I started that day, walking straight on was to go steadily back in time, because the children's quarter is discrete, complete: one narrow, chronological, all-spaces-occupied section that spans thirty years, from 1962 to 1992, when the tiny graves reached a driving path and had to stop. Thereafter, children, the Roselawn minority that they should be, were worked in among their elders.

No matter a few fresh mums, the children's hamlet, compared with the whole adult necropolis beyond, unquestionably exudes a forlorn and pitiful air. It is the orphan Roselawn, cold haven of children who orphaned their parents. The temporary metal markers are old, fallen, and nosing beneath the grass—trying to belie the full count of 150 graves. The decorated plots are simultaneously more intense and more derelict—built of rawest grief that blazed, consumed, and, perhaps blessedly, burned itself out. Is it shameful or healthful that a baby dead thirty years is finally left alone? Is it possible to mourn, forever, pure possibility?

Handmade headstones are more common here, crude in a way that seems fitting. They are childlike, emotional, spontaneous. To honor Kenneth Lee

Pollock, who lived one day at precise midsummer, someone nailed boards to two posts, carved his name and an arrow-pierced heart in deep grooves, and hammered the whole into the dirt: a rustic signpost of love and death. Its cement counterparts, offering more valentines, lie nearby. A heart headstone juts up at right angles from a painfully short slab bearing Michael Dean Hollar's name and span (Nov 5 73, Dec 10 74). It is as though "Mom, Lisa, and Jamie" yielded with abandon to the temptation of a still-wet sidewalk— signing their names with "love," reminding us that "God needs little angels too." In Darrel Duwayne Strickland's liquid rock, the bereaved swirled graffiti hearts, now forever stiffened. One heart holds the space of his life, gone before a year was out, on the eve of a new one.

SEPT. 27 ♥ DEC. 31

Perhaps these families couldn't afford a store-bought stone. But perhaps they simply couldn't wait. A stone takes time. People don't go in the ground one day and receive their solid tribute the next, at least not without meticulous planning—something hard to imagine for a child, even a child parents know they are losing. No, I like to believe the Pollocks, Hollars, and Stricklands wanted to do it quickly and do it themselves. Which is not to say the high-end clown headstones here (standard model, personalized message) are not equally loving and agonized. Isn't it good that parents, numb or distraught, can go to the monument merchant—a trip they expected their child to make for them—and find a clown holding balloons, a cheery bright-colored Bozo their baby would have laughed at? Small comfort, yet something. A thing.

Grief has no formula. Somehow this grief least of all. Why do the twins Dawn and Tonia Roddenberry (Nov. 24, 1972) lie together forever beneath a single granite headstone, within a boxwood hedge for a crib? Why do Christopher Gueltzow and James E. Gueltzow have only funeral-home plaques, only the month of birth/death noted (Nov 1983), and yet a guardian statuette between them of a boy carrying a goose?

And who is Jane January that the Tallahassee Police Department would bury her and then let ants pile a foot-high mound at her head? I do not chastise them. The burying was a long time ago, the first day of January 1980; and perhaps it is a fitting Roselawn irony for ants to boil and roil beside a stone inscribed, "Step softly. A dream lies buried here." These officers ached and acted. Isn't Jane January a better burial name than Baby Jane Doe? Was she a bathroom baby? A trash can child? A premature casualty in a New Year's wreck?

Or a cop's kid.

Whoever she was or would have been, the sad slab, "erected" by the police, is part of a little shrine where a squirrel, a bear, a duck, a dog, a clown watch over Jane January, and her chilly dreams.

This part of Roselawn compresses three decades' fashions in naming. John, Michael, and Elizabeth—like Jane—remain timeless. The sixties-seventies cusp favored Eric, Lisa, and Melissa (no hippie Rain or Chastity here); the eighties-into-nineties brought Justin, Ashley, Joshua, Megan, Brandy, Brett, and Blair. Any child's name—lovingly discussed and chosen, meant to be stenciled and embroidered on belongings—must, incised in stone, in some measure mock the namer. And what of the parents who waited nine months for Justice? Who expected Eden? Beautiful, bitter names.

Scattered

The toys here show fashions too (along with bizarre juxtapositions: angels snuggled up to tanks). I'm thrown back to Lance's babyhood by cute animal figurines, unbroken all these years, and rag dolls, recognizable through rot. I have only to go to the other children's corner, the live one, to get my hands directly on this difference.

I become The Secret Toy Thrower. One day, kids gone, I noticed a large cage inside the play-yard fence and suspected pet rabbits. Shamelessly skulking close, I indeed saw rabbits, running water, and, to my delight, fat white doves. They didn't look so delighted. They looked pooped, as if from not flying. By this time, I had clambered through root thickets, swatted aside stringy azalea branches, and found precarious purchase on dirt mounds, all the while marveling at the plastic inventory tossed over the fence. Either the teachers didn't know (unlikely) or had stonewalled retrieval (more likely).

"Well, Thaddeus, guess you don't have a shovel now. I'm very sorry." (Yeah, right.) "Remember our rule? Over the fence—bye-bye."

Enough shovels had gone bye-bye to dig a kiddie escape tunnel. Anyway, there I was, there were the toys. I heaved a few back inside. Then a few more. Then I couldn't stop. I followed the Trail of Toys all the way back to the far end of the property—discovering more play lots and pet cages, fascinated with my booty, imagining (I'll admit) the kids' coming wonderment at this overnight abracadabra. And they would notice. They left their playground clean, and their missiles had been flying out for months. I redeposited: three blue shovels, two yellow, one red, one green; four red buckets, two green, two yellow; fluorescent orange watering can; green rake; green McDonald's rake decorated with veggie characters (Mr. Bean, Miss Corn, etc.—Mr. Pickle Chip conspicuously missing); telephone receiver; blue basketball (collapsed); gold foam ball; yellow tennis ball; red ball; orange ball literarily labeled "Walcott/DuBose"; green frisbee; yellow and white boat; toucan head with six-inch orange beak; two huge coffee cups, perhaps flung by nerve-jittered teachers getting in the spirit.

I may never again refling such a bonanza. The Secret Thrower still stalks, but subsequent rescues have been lighter, a shovel here two buckets there. How queer do you think it that I wrote down every rake? Empiricism seized me because the toys, the whole scene, struck me funny. I certainly wasn't looking for lessons, to be induced from a list of playthings. Yet here I am, picking them up all over again, and finding, in the end, that the catalogue is its own induction: abundance, exuberance, a helter-skelter path of primary-colored plastic (heavily oriented toward sowing one's oats), busy, busy, bright, and abandoned.

Winged, Wounded

So because Roselawn's lost children can't scatter their own toys, their parents have. Some mementoes on the graves, though vintage, could be outside the school fence: tractors, Tonka trucks, dolls. The most frequent burial toy, though, never is: angels.

Kneeling, standing, praying, kissing; boys and girls alone, together; carrying lambs and birds; wearing crowns of pastel roses, golden wings, golden braids, and blue off-shoulder blouses. A few are really fairies, though clearly meant for angels. Fairies of paradise. It doesn't matter, for they are winged children, wee sprites, beings who all believe have flown straight to heaven. The headstones tell us.

WELCOME ALL ANGELS.

I LOST A DAUGHTER,
WITH GOD'S HELP I NOW HAVE AN ANGEL.

GOD NEEDS LITTLE ANGELS TOO.

WHAT IS HEAVEN WITHOUT CHILDREN?
LITTLE ONES TO HIM BELONG.

ANOTHER LITTLE ANGEL BEFORE THE HEAVEN.
WE WILL MEET AGAIN.

TREAD SOFTLY AN ANGEL LIES HERE.

A CHILD OF GOD

Amid the host of time-tarnished cherubs stand out some so brilliantly white I thought they had been placed by other hands—a recent visitor who, for whatever reasons, wanted to sow newer, cleaner angels. But they're not new. I see it's just a trick of the smooth, high-gloss ceramic from which these inches-high busts are made. No dirt clings, which is exactly right. For these are the graves of the unsullied, the ones who, unlike us dusty, mud-splattered creatures, have had no chance to be coated with earth's dirt. They are under it and out of it. They are still pure and fortunate—and deprived.

What wrenches so about these deaths wrings my mind. Children's simplicity may be a quality we all treasure, but our response to it is anything but. If Wordsworth were wholly right, we would not mourn dead children. And we know he is partly so, because in his intimations of immortality we recognize ourselves, what we have been and are.

> ... trailing clouds of glory do we come
> From God, who is our home:
> Heaven lies about us in our infancy!
> Shades of the prison-house begin to close
> Upon the growing boy,
> But he beholds the light, and when it flows,
> He sees it in his joy;
> The youth, who daily farther from the east
> Must travel, still is Nature's priest,
> And by the vision splendid
> Is on his way attended;
> At length the man perceives it die away,
> And fade into the light of common day.

Why should we anguish that a young soul regains the splendid, luminous vision? Of course we do, and keenly. Sometimes I think our pain is guilt: Here is a child, a total innocent, going through the pain and death we know should be our lot. More emotions, too: rage; and simple, sad regret for what these interrupted beings will never know.

Irrepressible, Episcopal Liz had one caveat about

Gordon's service, which she emphatically expressed to Kerry, Andrea, and me (and somewhat more diplomatically—maybe—to her priest): "I told him to say whatever he felt, but that if I hear even a whiff of 'Everything always happens for the best,' I'll be on my feet with 'Excuse me!'"

Life isn't a prison-house, at least not an unrelieved sentence. No matter how harsh or fallen or unfair this daily world, most of us, most of the time, don't want to leave it. Life hurts, it infuriates, it scalds, but it also blesses with its own naked glories. Life is; we are. And we know dead children are cheated. They have no possibility not to be innocent, to fall into common, extraordinary day.

Liz miscarried two children between Connor and Logan, her children with her second husband, John. The first one was only weeks along; the second, unmoving inside her, so much beyond that she had to deliver it after induced labor. I saw her grieve as I never had. Perhaps a time had to come when Liz's flood gates opened, after all her horrors: father murdered, mother self-killed, my beloved mother lost, Gordon gone. I stayed with her for two days soon after the miscarriage, soon enough that she was still exhausted from anaesthesia. We took a good walk (which later she hardly remembered) and then she needed to nap in the hammock. After a while I came quietly back and saw with surprise, and a pang, that she was already awake, silently crying. "I don't understand," she said. She lay there so slight and vulnerable, her whole body and voice combining apology, bafflement, and pain. "I am so sad. I can't get my old defense mechanisms to work."

When I told Gary her words, he said one: "Good."

Not that he wished for her suffering or didn't hope for its end or wanted a Liz without her irreverent spontaneity. Yet Liz, no matter how young and how often she had competently risen to tragedy, was entitled to utter nakedness, which he knew. This loss became the black event her black humor couldn't shade. She grieved long, so long that friends not so delicately suggested counseling. How could such emotion be given to someone—if a someone—she never knew? They didn't understand.

Her body did. John did. She sat in a restaurant with him, a baby cried, and her milk came in. For nothing. Granted that Liz had an accumulation of reasons for heartache, yet a child or infant's death can unleash an ache of frightening fervor. So we come again to the children's corner, to a stone more cryptic even than Jane January's, a wild stone.

KNOWN BY HIM 680
BEAUTIFUL UNBORN CHILDREN
GOD FORGIVE US!

Zachary Earnest Eckert, "Whom God Remembers," is buried here with his mother's message, "I Love You, Mommy." Yet child, mother, and their bond are relegated, graphically insignificant, to the lower righthand corner. Balancing them, upper left, is a clean white statuette of Mary and son, set unattached on the stone. The centerpiece of the highly polished granite is the crazy cry. What else can I call this wail? Its text cannot be translated into another, into mine, into anyone's other than Mommy's. She knows whether HIM is Jesus, God, or an abortion doctor. She knows how to unlock, though never in our logic, the secret significance of 680. She knows how sharply US is meant to pierce her, Zachary, me, you. In the end, all I can draw from this stone is passion. Fanatical passion. I am writing this thinking that Liz will bridle simply at proximity to an unhinged woman who hints at abortion as evil. As a midlife mother, Liz could face the possibility of aborting a fetus doomed to horrible defects. She did face horrible suffering when an almost-baby died inside her. Is such a woman, if she ever chose abortion, subsumed in the epithet *Murderer!*? No. Antiabortion obsession can flower into its own evil. Yet, in pacing through Roselawn's little lost ones, in troubling over how they confound us, I unexpectedly find this obsession a little less opaque. Is its spring, somewhere deep, the accusers' own terror and confusion—about life, about death—transformed into a crusade? We are not in control. We do not know how long we will exist above ground before disappearing beneath it. We do know that a child's death batters us bluntly with our helplessness.

But also with pure sorrow. To know what light has been extinguished, only walk across Roselawn, where, like a balance weight, the living children play.

Transfixed, Transformed

I didn't tell you why I led Andrea, Liz, and Logan to the nursery. We looked at the bunnies. We looked at the doves. We came to the cage at the far end, and, out of one jet eye, a golden pheasant looked at us.

I would never have found it if I hadn't followed the scattered line of playthings. A catch of breath, *Oh!*, all the emotional delight that physically floods me whenever a new, shy, or beautiful bird blesses my eyes: I felt every bit of this familiar gift but the shock of more. In the presence of a golden pheasant, it is impossible not to feel paltry. Wonder-struck— especially to come upon one hidden in a rough cage, with only two nervous rabbits as an audience for its slow-motion strut. Not obsessive birders, my sisters and Logan nevertheless shared a speechless instant (not unlike the start on sight of Otis' Technicolor bus, minus the laughter).

This bird is fabulous, in person and in story. All of its colors are richly royal: yellow gold, ruby red, midnight blue, black. That first day, I didn't know what I was looking at, except glory. It is a bird whose luxuriant feathers seem a cloak, an emperor's cloak made by a magical tailor who has conjured jewels into silk. Its whole head and crest are a gold of liquid sun. Its throat is collared with the delicate striping—black and gold, then blue and gold—that Fra Angelico wisely stole for his angels' wings. Its breast is fire. Its wings are a blue of deep sky and deeper water. Its tail, its two feet of tail, is a miraculous, single-quilled, spotted sweep of black and gold, graced with red, that splits finally into plumes.

I found it pictured (head only) under "Exotics" in Peterson's field guide. I found it again in a dictionary of symbols. The golden pheasant is the phoenix.

Why does this particular pheasant live in the far corner of Advent Episcopal Day School play yard? Who, surely awestruck, had to have it? Who now tends it—with what grumbling or reverent spirit? What do the children do with it except ignore it, all novelty past? What does it dream of, swinging on its huge plastic PlaySkool perch?

Someday I may answer these questions, though only the pheasant can satisfy the last. For now, the bird is its own wordless revelation, beauty so unexpected and excessive the miraculous hovers into human life—even inside chicken wire, over a square of dingy sand. The golden pheasant isn't a quiescent image of peace, like the dove. It is extreme, fierce, a bird the Chinese believe becomes a snake and whose loud wings make it the thunder bird. In fables its cry presages supernatural disaster. In myth it never dies. It dies into life.

The children don't know they play next to the Urphoenix. Nor did I at my first startled sight. Nor must we to feel its sensuous spiritual promise. The dirty little girls and boys. The pristine angels. The unbelievable bird. The squeals and laughter, the powerful cry, the silence. I haven't the words, I haven't the verbs, to unite them in ultimate solace. Something, though, brings them together at Roselawn; I live listening to them all.

CHAPTER 5

Wild Kingdom

Ants were the harbingers of home ownership on Brookmont Drive. They attacked my feet, on the walkway, before I set foot inside. Some omens we choose to ignore.

Gary and I saw this house on the first day we set out with our long-suffering realtor. Its emotional pull was immediate, but ... You can imagine the *but*'s on Day One, when we still believed in ticking off each item, to mutual satisfaction, on our low-cost, dream-home shopping list. (Andrea likes remembering the day—not One—when she asked how the hunt was going, and I said, "Oh, we've decided not to get a house. We're getting a divorce instead.")

Six months, seventy-five houses, miles of hideous wallpaper, and the realtor's dimming perkiness later, we said, "Let's go back to Brookmont." The ants bit me again. Big deal. It's Florida. Insects rule. We bought the house, wallpaper and all.

Not that we accomplished this without trauma. Gary managed a rite-of-berserkness before any major life change involving fine-print, big-bucks debt. Ants, though, were not involved. They did not raise their myriad ravenous heads again for weeks—or Gary would have added them to his post-inspection list of reasons to back out, which included a low attic (crowded with, *surprise!*, rafters). Panic subsided; the closing closed.

Promptly a good omen, the bluebirds, appeared. I saw them, or thought I did, before we took possession, when I kept driving past the house like a besotted betrothed. From a bush, a blurry rush flashed *bluebirds* into my brain. This is a mysterious moment to me still. Having never seen a bluebird—still a diminished species in our area—nor knowing of them in town, I discarded my intuition as a wishful hallucination. But I was right. Soon a neighbor, seeing me stroll with binoculars, asked with Welcome Wagon pride, "Have you seen our bluebirds?"

They are Roselawn's bluebirds, really. My neighbor didn't credit it, but the cemetery is the draw: its open spaces, its insects—grasshoppers being the specific foodchain delicacy. Now my bird reading came back to me. Because bluebirds want wide open spaces, they are electric-blue haunters of graveyards. And the males are thrillingly, heartbreakingly blue. Bluebirds prosper now in Roselawn, more each year, but that inaugural summer they remained elusive, rare.

Meanwhile, I was wishing they relished ants. We had a feast of them. Well, that's putting it backwards. I now know that under our property lay (and still lies) a Universe of Ants in which our home was merely one well-stocked palace on the queen's royal route. Barren and crumbless during the change of owners, it fell from favor. The ants bided their time. We moved in. The bacchanalia began anew.

The traps left in all the cabinets should have been a clue. I thought they were for roaches, a foe every Floridian expects. Yes, everyone has ants too. But how many of you have experienced, upon reaching for Kahlua from the high shelf, a rain of ants upon your head? Sheets of ants, snaking squadrons of ants. Ants piloting—unseen, effortlessly—the palace's labyrinthine catacombs: under its slab, along its pipes, inside its walls, out its electric sockets.

"Piss ants," offered the exterminator, among more scientific labels. He was professional, concerned, calm, but I saw the glee. Here was a dream case, the mother lode. Control slipping, "Ant INFESTATION!!" he frothed on the inspection report. After getting his astronomical Swat Team estimate, we chose instead a local company unencumbered with national advertising campaigns, and I got to know "the bug man" well, until his treatments (which he knew I hated) finally pissed off the little pissers. Now the ants mostly pop up to sun themselves by the pool—and to remind me that their universe will always and forever encompass (and undermine) ours, bug persons or no.

Watching how much ants love to embrace the hard edges of human habitation—sidewalks, the pool's concrete apron, grave slabs—it is tempting to blame the extraordinary INFESTATION!! on Roselawn and its stones. Maybe I can't, but nevertheless, between the bluebirds and the ants, I was aware early of Roselawn as a sanctuary for what we biped usurpers now call "urban wildlife." So for a long time I noticed the real animals living in the cemetery more than the fake ones. Of course when Gary and I moved in, we weren't faced, upon turning left out of the gate, with two near-lifesized deer butts. They loped in later.

Home, Home

The two deer, a buck and a doe, are quite a cemetery statement, stealing thunder even from Otis. Except that someone keeps stealing their tails, and now the buck's antlers. The pair is both buck- and butt-naked. (Resolving, in at least one instance, the fascinating linguistic debate over usage of these useful terms.) My sharp-eyed friend Peggy saw these deer on TV recently. She recognized them instantly, especially as the un-tails were the breaking story. When the deer first arrived, I thought the tails broke off by themselves. The poor buck mooned me almost immediately; there his tail lay, on the ground. *Flaw-in-the-naturalistically-painted-concrete*, I thought. The McGlamory family performed an emergency epoxy operation: on again. Off. On. Off. Gone.

Then hers gone.

Then horns gone.

The newscast confirmed the vandalism. Whether the news day was desperate, the reporter really moved, or Roselawn a top-of-the-mind topic after Governor Lawton Chiles's sudden death and burial (near the deer), the station seized the family's plight for a story. Art-historian Peggy, who makes Roselawn rounds with me and Barb sometimes, and who makes life livable by laughing at it, couldn't help being amused at the sudden fame of our nonfurry friends. But she knew the family's distress was real; besides, she added with a swift but firm look, "I *like* the deer."

I do too. They stand side by side, looking at the parallel graves of a husband and wife, and looking as if they belong. Whatever the specific associations of deer for the McGlamorys, this pair seem benevolent, watchful spirits: alert yet gentle, frozen yet graceful. Great sculpture they're not, but too tacky they're not. I realize I feel the same warring pulls the Wallace bus-tribute elicits. Yes, two big deer standing sentinel over dead people inch close to the comic. Yes, they're also a gift of honor—a literal concretization of love.

I saw some of the McGlamory family once, live, not televised. I was so concerned not to ogle that I missed whether pin-the-tail-on-the-deer was transpiring. But I saw that this was an occasion, a site visit as well as a pilgrimage. The children installed the deer only after their mother's recent death, when she joined, once more, their father. The cutting of her name and the placing of her slab put into place the last piece of a huge piece of their lives. And what they wanted, as do all of Roselawn's more ambitious developers, was not just a place for bodies but a *place*: an existence, not an exit. So the McGlamorys now perpetually reside in a symbolic meadow—with domesticated deer. I wouldn't have chosen (or paid for) these conspicuous pets; but now I would miss them, as I most definitely do their tails.

More Equal Than Others

Animal effigies are everywhere in Roselawn, both carved into stones and set on ground or slab in the form of yard ornaments, whimsical planters, door stops (a dachshund), and toys. In most cases, as with the deer, the impulse is the comfort of the pastoral, the peaceable kingdom. Obviously, people choose animals they, or their loved ones, loved—or loved to hunt. The paradox isn't one to many people. I've never handled a gun in my life and can't imagine drawing a bead on a deer, but I have known hunters who revel in nature quite as much as in their blood sport. They revere the creatures they stalk. The cement fawns lying curved at the feet of graves, the cute bunnies, and the doves bearing branches don't, one can reasonably assume, represent targets. But the leaping stags and the leaping bass probably do. The young north Florida men laid out prematurely in Roselawn, squinting forever beneath billed caps (or as long as their plasticized color photos last), took comfort both in the woods and the trophies they took away. One stone even memorializes weapons: a rifle and a pistol. But these men could have been the accidental prey. It happens every hunting season. Would a wife or parent celebrate in stone what the hunter loved, even when it killed him? Perhaps. Living contradictions is one of the ways humans live at all. (I am having a flash of myself in a restaurant this week, ravenously eating quite dead fish while oohing and aahing over brilliant sea creatures in elaborate aquariums.)

Carnivore or vegetarian issues aside, peace in nature is a definite headstone theme: the seven-year-old boy fishing with his dog beside him; the couple walking on a shore; a deer drinking from a lake; two graceful swans touching bills (love birds); two brightly painted, foot-tall, cock and hen figurines (good country couple). Mary and Joseph are more common than St. Francis—I have found two statuettes, one with birds and squirrels set at his feet—but animals outnumber any other image, even angels I think. The Franciscan associations are what most people invoke: the protection of the innocent, the delight and consolations and lessons of nature. On the back of an eighteen-year-old boy's headstone, a mother prays her son will "be a free bird like he always dreamed of."

Domestic pets are present too, of course. Some are as generic as the stags and doves: saccharine kittens and long-haired cats; concrete hounds with flower baskets between their teeth (seeing a row of these at a local garden center recently gave me a disoriented split second; oh well, planting is planting). Some, I imagine, symbolize personal canine friends: a boxer, a bull dog, a bassett, a poodle reading a book and holding a quill pen. One, I suspect, though only a name on a rock ("Kibbie") is actually interred beside his master. People and their pets. Knowing several people (including blood relations) who proclaim, somehow sheepishly *and* feistily, "You know the truth? I like dogs better than people," I would be very surprised if Roselawn contained only one four-footed friend.

So even before I read the article about monuments for pets in our local paper, I found myself wondering: Would animals' headstones feature people—a boy throwing a stick, a man reclined in a La-Z-Boy, a woman can-opener in hand? The story didn't say. The owner of the local pet-headstone business acknowledged the controversy of her enterprise. People were either offended or grateful. (Or, like petless me, bemused and amused.) One thing was clear in the article, the full range of human burial tastes is extrapolated to animals. And why wouldn't it be? From "Kibbie" on a rock to dog casket pillows and blankets. Fish and frog caskets. Animal-shaped cremation urns. Double-walled caskets that can be moved when the owner does. (Tallahassee has no pet cemetery—yet.)

I am not scoffing at this bereavement. Death first became real to me when, at ten, I watched my dog "put to sleep." I didn't do well. I shocked the vet and myself by seizing the body and clinging, to absolutely no effect, for dear life. I see my blind lunge was a shadow moment, a diluted pre-image, of my father's death-stun: my body acting before my brain caught up.

But despite these deep personal attachments to pets—or perhaps because of them—most animals watching over Roselawn's dead are wild. And some weird. Lambs, birds, fawns, rabbits, squirrels one expects. Raccoons and foxes maybe. Pelicans perhaps. Pigs, turtles, snails . . . let's presume the bestowers liked the fanciful figurines, not the bestiary metaphors.

Logan's favorite grave when he was a toddler (and had no idea it was a grave) is marked only by a metal plaque and a circle of cartoonish woodland critters: several small painted foxes, squirrels, hares, and raccoons, all in different poses, ready to join paws in a ring dance. "Oooh," he said every time he toddled upon it. Then he squatted, stared, and smiled—feeling exactly what Garrett Thomas Kelley Burton's parents knew he would have, if among the animals, not under them.

Someone put one of these cute raccoons on Governor

Chiles's grave, to represent his infamous description of himself as "the old he-coon." (I won't count, as an animal tribute, the plot's Wild Turkey bottle containing a feather.) Picture yard gnomes and you have the raccoon's genre. Picture, in fact, Sleepy, Grumpy, Doc, or Dopey. They could appear any day in Roselawn. Dumbo, Mickey, and Minnie already have.

Now there's a theme park waiting to happen: Disneylawn. It won't happen here, though. Roselawn is already too defined and, despite the occasional odd or droll gracenote, too real, even rural. A purely human construct it may be, but the graveyard is an animal habitat, an in-town oasis like any park. One of the pleasures of living next door is that real creatures scurry, slink, crawl, and fly among their molded counterparts, oblivious to their immortalization as funereal art. No Dumbos, deer, sheep, or pigs (unless admirably secretive) gad about—but possibly a fox does. I've longed for a sighting since I heard the rumor of "our fox" from, naturally, my bluebird source.

Where Is Thy Sting?

I found the bees on my own—and wish I were the only one who had. For a while the hive, in the base of a big oak (and about as picturesque as Walt could have animated it), probably was my secret. The tree grows just off Roselawn's southeast curve, as the path drops past the culvert and toward the grass slope. You have to step up, off the road, to see the bee's entrance, a neat triangle that, when the bees were busiest, was solid with squirming, humming workers. They fascinated me, massing there, doing something purposeful and important, though appearing merely to jostle one another, like too many people pressing into a stadium. Honey was their goal. And since honey is a twice-daily part of my tea ritual, I looked on them with vicarious gratitude. My paw wouldn't be stuck in that particular honeypot, but it spoons out other bees' stolen sweetness all the time.

I knew, theoretically, that they wouldn't sting me if I didn't interfere; after a few visits I was convinced. Workers buzzed by me, in and out, intent only on the Task. I even magnified them with binoculars, from four or five feet away, marveling at their pollen coats. Then I mostly left them to it, only now and then checking activity when I was walking my green routes. Months of peaceful industry went by, and then I found a crumpled soft drink can thrown near the hole; then rocks, more trash, spray paint. This is another area where workers sometimes park equipment, and I'll never know whether they (with misplaced industry) or kids did the damage, but someone couldn't bear to let the bees *be*. Finally a knotty stick was jammed into the entrance and the hive gone. Dead, fled, I don't know. The random malice dumbfounded me, but a friend said maybe, in the end, it was the crew's fear: *Can't have bees swarming through the cemetery!* Maybe. More likely it was that human venom: meanness.

Anyway, Logan and his older brother Connor got to see the hive while it thrived. They both love bugs, even the ones Aunt Ellen can't call up any anthropomorphic love for (slick caterpillars). It was a good nature day. I mentioned rabbits before we left the house, and lo, one bounced up. Away, rather. Logan had been exhausting me and Liz with his skating exploits, which involved — in these safety-conscious times — the interminable preskating gear-fitting (knee pads, elbow pads, wrist bands, of which only he had the mysterious power to know left from right); the choosing of the steepest, not the nearest, hill; the decision to wobbly-walk to it because smooth skating was harder than it looked; and the brilliant idea to whiz effortlessly down between mother and aunt, each little hand clasped to a running relation.

Liz and I came to tough-love time: *If the gear fits, fall down in it. We provide moral support only.* Logan took it well, and anyway I remembered the bee hive and set us all toward it, some distance away. Just then I saw a white tail-flash, yelled "Rabbit!," and both boys shot off—Logan unbelievably running uphill in skates, following Connor, who had also seen the cottontail and kept shouting sightings, "There it is!"

"Where?" wailed Logan.

"There! There!" Connor had become bunny, zigzagging on a dime, a feat the wheeled one could not keep up with. You would think these boys lived in a concrete jungle devoid of fauna, instead of on a perfect little silver-dollar lake where hawks and herons perch in backyard trees. (In fact, on my last visit there, I looked out the sliding glass doors and ran breathlessly to Connor in the kitchen: "There's a *huge* black pig in the backyard!" Which there was. Connor didn't even look: "Oh. Sally." Sally resides a few houses over and periodically escapes—no doubt curious about the next delicacy the boys will feed her, on that occasion Cheddar Cheese Combos.)

A Sudden Blow

Yet the cemetery is not only new to my nephews, but special, a respite from my suburban streets, rabbit-possible.

Logan never saw one that day, a disappointment that diminished interest in the bees, which he perfunctorily perused. A bunny tail became his white whale. I sympathize, having left my bed one warm night to chase a barred owl's hoots into the cemetery and back into Allie's yard (a trespass showing my mania). I came to my senses, realizing I was a 911 call in the making, but the owl was *so close*. It tantalized me right outside the bedroom window but kept stealthy when I pursued. You have only once to be swooped by an owl's wide wings, as I was when Gary and I camped in New Mexico, to keep imprinted the powerful thrill. Sometimes it's freely given. Barred owls do come abroad in day, often at dusk. I saw one sitting, like a gigantic songbird, in a neighbor's spare-branched tree, bottom limb. Perhaps owls refuse to be the prey, even of a puny, flightless person. I know someone who talks back and forth to a barred owl nightly, mimicking its barking-dog mating call, but it too revealed itself only on its own terms, in one frightening pass. Stalking it produced nothing.

So I wait to be caught unaware. Roselawn is one great gift of birds. Crows congregate, as if they know their place. I first saw here a shrike, the butcher bird of Roethke's poem, a small murderer far more treacherous than the midnight crows. In our mild winters, mixed masses of songbirds often alight, the familiar titmice, nut hatches, and chickadees consorting with bluebirds and migrating warblers—snow birds that Florida birders don't want to send home. The hoary, snag-rich oaks are woodpecker hotels, riddled with nesting holes. Sometimes I hear the unmistakable, tropical call of the pileated woodpecker (Woody) or its equally identifiable resonant pecking. This chicken-sized bird *pecks*, its gorgeously red-crested head thumping bark like an elegant jack hammer. About a week ago, though, I saw one eating dirt. Clay to be precise, the clay at the slope bottom. To see this magnificent bird down on my lowly level was a wonder in itself. The curious behavior was another. He let me watch for a long time, from several yards away. Without field glasses, I don't know really whether he was eating. I do know from my owl communer, Stephen, that one species of equatorial birds has learned to eat clay as an antidote to something unsavory in their diet. Also, it's nesting time now, so perhaps the clay was meant for home improvement.

This sighting was extraordinary, but every single walk yields something—if I'm looking. Or at least open. My walking has always been mostly about movement, taking steps, covering ground. A naturalist I'm not. But at some point, long ago in the old neighborhood, I realized that some small surprise is always *there*. Always. A tree, a rock, a cloud. A cat killing a squirrel.

Now sometimes, especially as I've become bird batty, I actively look. After Stephen once showed me, during a stroll, that almost every big bush in Roselawn held a nest, I took Logan on a similar expedition. This was his weekend to stay here without mom and dad—a big event for both of us. After the first few discoveries—Logan's round blond head poking in as I held parted branches—he raced from gardenia to camellia shouting, "Hey, Aunt Ellen! *Here's* one!" Little did we know we'd started our outing with the biggest surprise. I've put a bluebird box on one of Roselawn's pines not far from my gate. (Boxes, feeders, and bird baths are among the plot landscapings in the cemetery, but anything needing daily tending is derelict soon enough. No matter how much the griefstricken want this new place to be a home, it isn't. Not for them, anyway.) I hadn't seen Mr. and Mrs. in and out of the box for a while, so before Logan and I set out wandering, I unscrewed the box's side and lifted out the pine-straw nest, setting it by the trunk.

Roselawn is a big place for little legs, especially if they're on a nest hunt. Logan flagged long before he admitted it, only because the subtext of his quest was . . . rabbits. They wouldn't oblige. So we headed home. Passing back by the bluebird tree, it occurred to me that mulching it with the discarded nest might offend future families, so with Logan watching, I pitched the straw—a high, compact block—away. Out of its arcing orbit flew five powder blue eggs. Out of my mouth flew, "Oh my God." Here we were, the great bird lovers home from the hills, tossing bluebird nests with abandon and scrambling the eggs. Only one, as it turned out. I hadn't a clue what to do but put everything back, not terribly compactly. Logan followed all this with fascination, especially the exquisite eggs.

Eventually one of them became his. After breeding season, I opened the box and there they all were. I blamed myself, though I'd found unhatched eggs at other times. Only recently I read that a fair percentage of bluebird eggs don't hatch—and that sometimes parents build second nests right on top of their first.

That high nest. Those hidden eggs. Ah.

This cemetery box opens to me more than its share of revelations. The last azure jolt was a dead male, all alone, unmarked, in the bare box. I doubted my eyes and stood there a dumb thing. I felt as you might if objects could materialize, whole, in any place and time of your ordinary life. Walk into the bathroom and find a cannonball on the counter. Get into the car and discover a stiff squirrel in the passenger seat. Oh, the context wasn't bizarre; yet it was. I opened that box because we, people and birds, were already feeling spring. I thought simply to check for squatters, primarily huge nasty "palmetto bugs" (roaches), and their leavings. I, in my role as priestess of fertility rites, swung the door open on death. Breathtaking death. That bird was no one's prey and it had not been gone long. Heart attack? Cold? Bluebirds are known for susceptibility to freezing, and our eerily erratic February had taken a sudden dip below 32° after a warm spell so long all the flowers opened. In cold, bluebirds roost together overnight. Maybe he *didn't* die alone. And maybe he was weak, a Darwinian casualty. Earlier winter nights had been far colder.

I put him in the freezer. Let's be honest: When again would I be so close to one of these splendid creatures? And I was not above show-and-tell. So, briefly my home functioned as morgue for one of Roselawn's lost. I did feel decidedly queer for the twenty-four hours I knew my freezer held more than ice cream, spinach, vodka, hot dogs, and chicken breasts. Slightly ashamed, scandalously amused at the exotic poultry; Audubon gallows humor. All drollery ceased when I pulled some of his reluctant feathers. I *had* to do it. This beauty wasn't all meant to be buried. Now the rest of it is, under fuchsia azaleas in my back yard.

The death led me to the front yard too, to open the box I've put on another pine there. Roach poop never looked so good. No casualties. At the moment, in fact, a bluebird couple is working on their second brood. I had to lure these cemetery inhabitants to the house, patiently. For two seasons they teased me and Gary with box-inspections but let titmice move in. Other graveyard critters aren't so reluctant. Rabbits come through the hedges and munch gladiolas. A raccoon came to drink at first dark from rain water caught on the pool cover. A box turtle took a fancy to the pool itself one dry spring. Gary, finding it turtling along in the driveway, was enthralled with its tall domed shell, with its painted markings. I think it took him back to his ultrabrief Boy Scouting, his favorite memory of which was the river trip when his troop smashed three out of four canoes.

The turtle, he figured, was on a single-minded mission for water, but a plod toward the street was sure death. The cemetery, from whence it came, was the direction of life. So back it went, this time personally escorted through our gate. Days later, I looked out from the bedroom to see a plate-sized dead magnolia leaf being sucked slowly toward the pool's skimmer port. Well, Gary would fish it out of the catch-basket later. Yes, it was the box turtle. If I'd gone back to my office, instead of wandering out to the pool, it would have been caught, hidden, in the skimmer—a vortex of death for frogs, giant spiders, baby moles and baby birds, if we didn't find them in time.

The pool is a liquid magnet for other Roselawn wildlife, probably when runoff is scarce. One night I woke to bumps in the back yard. I lay stiff, waiting to see if they came again, jumpy because Gary wasn't there. More. Odd sounds. I couldn't just lie still, waiting for the ax murderer. I flipped the switch for the outside floods. There on the end of the diving board, caught in the spotlight, considering a dip, was a possum. It looked full at me—long enough for me to wonder, once again, why any nocturnal animal needs to be that ugly.

Snails may grace Roselawn's graves. Possums, uh uh.

Zero at the Bone

Which brings up snakes, spectacular to some, repellent to most. I'm with Emily. In all of our years on Sixth Avenue, I never saw a snake. The first two years here, they were everywhere: curled fatly under the oak, slithering away from an outside faucet, leaping straight up through a crack between deck boards (raising the hideous question: what was *chasing* it?), inching past my office window while I talked to an editor in Boston *(Are you serious? What kind?)*. Ugly kind.

An oak snake, as it turned out. They're grayish, silvery, bark-patterned constrictors, a word I associated only with horrific jungle snakes. Yes, well, I've now seen small-scale constriction, an educative moment I didn't need. But that came later. Like the ants, the house-warming snakes moved on, back to the cemetery I assumed, except that I've never seen one in Roselawn—a fact so improbable as to be conspiratorial. They're there.

I *put* one there. Or John did, at my service. After the long snake-free period, Satan moved in. His wiles were infinite, his appetites obsessive, his illusions complete, his escapes uncanny, his effrontery a tad too personal.

To take your seat for this miracle play, you must get inside my glass walls. Picture late-sixties ersatz Frank Lloyd Wright: whole exterior walls of glass "sliders"; low interior partitions that let you see into three rooms at once; in the living room a row of four big plate-glass windows; and in my office, the built-in bird window: an entire corner of glass, two panes five-and-a-half-feet high, joined at their right angle by nothing but glue and one small metal clip. We have an unobstructed view of the stage.

Of course I didn't see it as proscenium at first—except for the birds' amateur antics at the feeders and baths. One day from the kitchen, I glanced out the far living room windows and noticed a pine branch caught on the chains of the hanging bird bath. Tree debris is perpetual here. I would have plucked the branch the next time I refilled the bath or feeder, but luckily, later that afternoon, the branch crawled off by itself. And I saw it. The effect wasn't exactly cannonball-on-the-counter; more like opening the freezer to find my frozen blue friend pecking wienies.

Next morning the branch had redraped itself. Both novelty and repugnance were so strong I didn't want to *do* anything about the *trompe l'oeil* predator (no birds seemed fooled), so I showed it to passing neighbors, took a picture of it, and waited for it to move on. It did, to the next feeding station. The game was really on. I came through the side gate to the clear plastic feeder hanging outside my office window, at the opposite end of the house from the living room. Neatly coiled in the seed plate—nicely matching the grayish safflower husks—was my fiend. I tossed twigs at it, a laughable exorcism it ignored. Then, on the advice of an Indian acquaintance with much snake experience, I began to water it. She was right. Water was a good weapon, but unlike the Wicked Witch of the West, the snake was merely deterred, not dissolved. On its third return, Liz and John happened to be staying at the house.

Though John was already suited up for a late-morning meeting at the state Capitol, he was the only potential snake-handler around. Also, John admires snakes. Now I know snake lovers are right (you've heard them): snakes aren't slimy; they're fascinating; they're beautiful; they have their niche in nature; they're not lurking about looking to bite you.

My mind says yes; my nerve endings don't. Besides, this one was in *my* niche. When John teased me about my cruel water torture and snakes' rights, he asked for it: "All right, you catch it and give it a better home." He did. I was impressed. Down to the cemetery we went, the snake now in a towel. As it turned out, he should have taken it along to the nest of legislators.

Enough days passed that I decided all was over. Then, sitting just as I am now, at the keyboard, I looked out the glass corner to find the shifty chameleon stretched out inches away, along a thick azalea limb. Not in the feeder. Not on its chain. Just lolling on the branch. With a lump in its interminable belly. Don't tell me this digestive display wasn't intentional.

I roared outside, turned the water full blast, seized my weapon, and cried, "Get ready to be blasted, buddy!" The innocent stranger standing fifteen feet from me, concealed by a shrub, quailed but didn't drop to the dirt. He was considering buying my neighbor Marge's house. Evidently, he reconsidered. I never saw him or his blanched wife again. Oh, I explained. "The snake, the birds, the lump, la la, ha ha, blah blah." We commiserated. Nevertheless, bullet-proof vests would have danced in that man's head every time I came in the yard.

The snake continued to taunt me, its apparitions unsettling but, I must admit, *interesting.* The attractions of evil. Standing at the kitchen counter one day, I was on the phone telling another bird-buggy friend, Nancy, all about the sneak—who had been absent a while—and in midsentence exclaimed, "There it is. Right now!" It chose that moment to appear again on the wide-window stage of its original performance. Later that day I drove to Nancy's for afternoon wine. The next day she had her own stalker. She accused me of delivering it.

One whole day I passed through the house—office to kitchen to family room to front door—innumerable times, registering that the long tube feeder outside the living room (next to the hanging bath) was all clumped with sunflower seeds. In the hot, rainy late-summer, when the birds eat less, the leftover seeds become a glob, a true pain to clean out. On one pass, I finally sensed something. A glob anomaly was coming to consciousness. I went into the room, up to the window, the front-row seat. That devious, plastic pest was knotted inside the tube. This serpent's wiles, apparently, leaned heavily toward posing as food.

That day, thoroughly repulsed and unnerved, I did nothing. Besides, I didn't know *what* to do. Finally I was provoked beyond reason. I attempted snake-handling. Actually, snake-raking. I now knew my foe was not a feckless hunter. I'd seen it strike and narrowly miss a twittering, skittery house finch. I'd also seen the lump—a hit. Days later when I saw the snake again, half in and half out of the feeder, its upper body undulating as though it could climb air, I rushed outside. I had had it. But I had no plan.

When I stood in the driveway, the feeder before me at eye level, I understood the snake's acrobatics. It was working. A captive finch, still alive, lay looped helpless in one coil. The snake squeezed; they swung there together. I watched; I couldn't watch. In the garage I grabbed a rake and a cardboard box, two ridiculous tools that at the time didn't seem so, especially if the snake didn't want to lose its coiled cargo. Still, I felt desperately silly before this proficient predator. As I should have. The speed.

I batted the snake to the ground, onto the messy leaf mulch under the azaleas. It thrashed awkwardly, but not as awkwardly as I, trying both to pin it under the rake tines and to keep wide away from its writhings. I counted on sluggishness, but almost as soon as the snake hit the ground, that finch was halfway in its mouth. How I do not know. From the coil to the mouth was a magical transition, a sleight of snake, frames snipped from the footage. And then the bird was gone. Greedy, greedy beast. *A crazed woman may be batting me with a rake, but a meal is a meal.* Also, the snake whipped better unknotted. Whip, prod, whip, prod. Poof. The villain vanished. In an instant, I was prodding nothing but dirt. That oak snake, trapped between me and the house, did not slither away. I would have seen a shot for freedom. The logical conclusions are: under leaves or down a hole. There were no holes, the leaves were patchy. But you can choose any explanation you like. I was there. No matter where the snake got to, its getting was a master magician's last cloak of smoke. Now you rake me, now you don't.

Red in Tooth and Claw

It went to Nancy's. I haven't seen the snake again, a long time now, and don't know whether I vanquished it or it me. After all, since the devil made me murderous, the curtain can come down. Nancy keeps the snake, christened Sir Harry Oakes (the scales *will* be lifted from her innocent eyes), at bay by keeping her feeders full. She claims I redelivered him via hubcap or axle. But as the crow flies, or the snake flees, the shortest route from my house to Nancy's is: of course, Roselawn.

Whether the stalker exited through my back gate or not, it surely knows its way around the cemetery. Because whatever vision I and the purchasers of cute stone animals prefer, any pastoral place is a killing field. If you want the bucolic without blood, head for Orlando. Not that cartoons don't run red today—or that Bambi's mother wasn't murdered decades ago, and over and over and over since. Children often occupy the wild kingdom more easily than we. Logan finally saw his rabbit. On one last walk into Roselawn, he headed through the gate while I dawdled in the back yard. An urgent call brought me, hurrying.

There in the middle of the grassy border he stood, pointing off toward the south and the bee tree, his voice thrilled: "Aunt Ellen, Aunt Ellen! I saw the rabbit—and it's in a dog's mouth!" From his amazed little face, I looked left full into another. The animal stopped, turning to give us an appraising once-over, absolutely self-possessed and superior, despite the dinner dangling from its mouth. We were many yards away, no threat; off it trotted toward someone's back-line bushes. It was small, with alert pointed ears, a rather bushy face, medium-to-long coat, of a tawny color brightening toward orange. I wondered how its owners would receive this little gift. I wondered how Logan would. Matter-of-factly, to my relief. He wasn't *glad* the bunny bought it, but he wasn't torn up and asked not a single question. Logan had three large yard dogs at home, I had to remember—three hyper-excited reasons I finally made Connor and Logan stop feeding Sally the coveted Combos. Tortured barking was their only outlet for obvious frenzy. Logan knew dogs hunted.

He forgot the drama when his parents returned, but I've been thinking about that rabbit dog for a year. I'd never seen it before. I haven't since. You may be way ahead of me: I say it's the fox.

Poor Bare Forked

Wild kingdom. We humans like to name kingdoms. I believe there's a subtle satisfaction in it, a saving—as though the classifying itself, our mental power of abstraction, sets us above and apart. Roselawn resists separations. A cemetery concentrates kingdoms. It keeps them before us. It forces us into them. It worries us with their blurring borders.

The Kingdoms of the quick and the dead.

The Kingdoms of heaven and hell.

The Kingdoms of animal, plant, and mineral.

Wait. Where are we in that tripartite division of all nature? Where else. In with the snake, in with the ants, in with the bluebirds, in with the deer.

The eaters, and the eaten too.

Worm food.

CHAPTER 6

Home

Gary's stone is perfectly plain. Standard issue granite—name, birth, death—as I believed he would have chosen. He didn't. Until the end, he thought it wasn't.

Probably you knew, long ago, the hole in this plot, the missing part, the absence withheld, the round character oddly flat. Too many *I*'s, not enough *we*'s. (*I am having a lot of trouble with pronouns*, I said to Kristy, who was twenty-nine when her father died. How strange that even speech was strange. I could not open my mouth without saying *we*, and every plural pierced. Who, after all, was *I?*)

Or perhaps you felt Gary didn't appear often in Roselawn—not like Barb, Liz, Logan. He's been there all along, on every walk, on every page.

Time

He moved through Roselawn too, in the nearly three years we lived here together. You can place him in the picture—tall, lean to skinny, bearded, auburn-haired without one strand of gray—with Otis, Mr. Britt, the Fulghum family, the tiny headstones in the children's corner. But Logan he knew for only two years; he never saw the pheasant or the snake; he couldn't walk with me and Barb because our walks were a weekly *we* she created when I needed one, badly.

Other inner films I have of Gary and Roselawn you haven't seen. Here is one, late summer, after his forty-ninth birthday. We are headed toward the not yet bee tree. Facing fifty is, as Gary captures with pithy irritation, "absurd." I understand, because I feel so full of life, so hopeful, with so much freedom before us. Therefore, I nag. Cheerful, crisp, and short nagging about smoking that for once he doesn't mind. I know and he knows that the fifteen years since his leukemia have been a gift. We were not supposed to be strolling through a cemetery; he was supposed to be in one. And for four years, he almost was. Yet so much time has passed that we, no strangers to death's surprises, have become complacent in our living. I will, I tell him, be extremely irked if after all his suffering and inexplicable resurrection, an addiction—not mutant blood cells—cuts short our absurd fifties. To my surprise, he tells me he has already cut his daily cigarettes dramatically.

By Christmas he is smoking as few as ten and planning to ask his oncologist, Jim Mabry, about a low-dose nicotine patch. By then, also, he has seen Dr. Mabry about bothersome pain at a rib, where Gary believes his huge splenectomy scar is catching and pulling. By then he has had an x-ray whose inconclusive reading worries him far more than he tells me. By January, when he goes to his study for the first time since the holidays, pain will not let him sit upright at his desk.

It wasn't leukemia or its ghostly scar. It wasn't lung cancer. It was mesothelioma, the deadliest cancer caused by asbestos, the most cruel cancer I have seen. It waited thirty years after his exposure to appear. It took him in three months. Three hallucinatory months. Life was never so concentrated, so dense, and so unmoored. Extreme illness does this, as too many of you know. It is all fear and waiting, driving urgency that cannot act.

Lapsed Time

Naming the horror took five full weeks. I have an image of health care as a crazy cosmos, an unstable universe of multiple suns—the diagnosticians, the oncologists, the surgeons, the pain managers, the radiologists, the pharmacists, the home health nurses, the disjointed hospital departments—around which the patients and families cluster in yearning orbits, attracted, repelled, then sent spinning toward a new center far, far in another galaxy that seems to gleam more brightly. The panicked planets need light; they crave it. But they want to rest in it, and they can come to hate these shifting suns.

No one and nothing was ever in charge, except pain. *Controlling pain.* It's a mantra now, a humane and realistic one, when there is no cure. Yet the phrase reveals this: pain is master. Science merely weakens its grip. And mesothelioma did grip Gary. It seized the whole cavity of his upper body—and squeezed. Once in the early weeks, already taking prescription painkillers, Gary rose from his recline on the couch, crumpled head to knees, and pled incredulously to no one, "What *is* this?" Soon we knew and feared the word *mesothelioma*, written on the radiologist's report. The oncologists weren't convinced. Mesothelioma, insinuating itself into the body's and organs' linings, is notoriously difficult to diagnose, and yet there was Gary's asbestos exposure: a one-year pipe factory job, in 1964, in college. Mesothelioma's latency period can be forty years. Still, we dared to hope and joke. Hadn't Mabry recommended Dr. Saint for exploratory surgery? Much better than Saint's partner, Dr. Hurt.

Before the surgery, though, no one really saw the depth of Gary's hurt but me. He managed to get to appointments; he didn't confess the full pain when he talked with Kristy and Ian long-distance; his descriptions to doctors lacked sufficient drama. But I watched him getting vague. He lost time, telling Kristy that events of last week happened yesterday. He was lucid when he ached. He took a pill. He nodded. He woke in agony. He restarted the cycle. The morning he was due at the hospital—two days early to get stronger drugs—we went through the cycle twice and might have done it all day. *Why are you waking me,* he accused, and I felt pure villain until he understood and struggled to get up.

Neither of us realized, until I tried to leave his hospital room that night, how physically bound we had already become. I could not cross the threshold. We had hardly been out of each other's sight for weeks. I know now that from the January day when Gary went from desk to bed, everything we did was a taking leave of each other; yet we were growing together, not apart. I forced myself home.

Kristy came for the surgery. Both she and her younger brother Ian lived three hours away, not far from Liz and John. Lance was across the continent in graduate school. Petite, lively Kristy was her father's friend, the night owl who sat up telling truth with him when the rest of the family had fallen over. Beer might be involved. Kristy was a nonflaky free spirit (archaeologist turned infant researcher, after a happy hiatus as bagel waitress): a young woman after Gary's hippie Ph.D. heart. She arrived for the surgery knowing her youthful dad could be very ill, but not knowing the worst possibility. We heard it from Dr. Saint.

Pass over the weeping. I cannot promise you, now, to blackout every extreme, but tearjerking is not my territory. Gary at least wasn't crying; he was the only one making us laugh. Anaesthetic delirium didn't dissipate his quirky wit; it quirked it up a notch. The scrambled tales he told us I don't remember, but until his fog cleared, Kristy and I glimpsed the wild ride of hilarious associations that fed his songwriting (maybe his therapy too—not to patients' faces). Then we started laughing with him, not at him. In response to some odd recitation, I began blathering an anecdote about the time Simone de Beauvoir fell on a mountain. Gary deadpanned, "Was it hurt?"

Finally he was struggling only with memory, not

reason, especially names. A flotilla of doctors had come in and out of his fog, delivering fragments of information and drifting out. Only Dr. Mabry was a familiar anchor. He, Kristy, and I sat around Gary's bed for a grave discussion. When Gary faltered over a name, I burst out laughing. Both doctor and daughter winced. How insensitive! (or hysterical). But I knew the doctor Gary was looking for. He had been forgetting and renaming Dr. Saint for two days. First he promoted him to Dr. Christ. That morning he had tried his memory again, failed, and said to me, "You know. The Righteous Brother."

We all needed the comic cleansing. The discussion, a dire one, went on. Even then, though, Gary didn't get it. As soon as he was out of surgery, he was put on an epidural morphine pump, the last stage for pain. So though he came to consciousness, keeping it came hard. Dr. Saint, Dr. Mabry, Dr. Wickstrum the radiation oncologist—all of them told and retold this clearly conscious, intelligent man his diagnosis. Every time, there was a sleep and a forgetting. Finally the moment came to me. In the middle of the night, while I lay on the cot in his room, I heard him mutter, "When are they going to figure out what this is?" He heard me crying, demanded *"Ellen. Tell me."* and heard his fate at last.

Borrowed Time

Everyone soon knew that more than Gary's wit was intact. So were his intellect, his stubbornness, his fury, his will. He discharged himself from the hospital. He couldn't take it any more: the fear of course, but also the hospital's chaotic staff parade, the patronizing nurses, the elusive doctors, the horrible morphine pump on a pole—glowing red digits meting out his salvation but taking over his mind. So he busted out. The head of the home health service knew a determined man when she saw one and promised a personal pump and its specialized drugs at home. Dr. Mabry came in to find his patient fully dressed, sitting in a chair, dispensing no charm, and proclaiming, "I can't rest here and I'm leaving"—and didn't argue.

Gary was so glad to see Roselawn. Kristy and I stood with him near the back gate, while he cheerfully admired the dancers also enjoying the sun. "Dancers? Where?" Kristy asked, suspending disbelief, both because her father seemed perfectly rational and because on that beautiful day, in a graveyard that was our park, someone—someone as happy as Gary— might have danced.

"Over there," he said, pointing off toward tombstones in the direction of the church. I looked seriously, through the pines, among the stones, but I could not conjure them. "See them? Look. It's the graveyard dance."

"Oh?" Kristy flowed with him, giving me a discreet glance, amused, shiver submerged.

"Oh, yes. In a circle." So pleased he was, so sure, so willing to let our myopia pass. Gary saw a great deal we didn't. That day, neither one of us even thought of contradicting him. We saw a doomed man elated to be home, elated to be walking outside, breathing air, seeing and touching the familiar. Gary stayed up until dawn, still high from hospital drugs and happiness, with Ian watching over him.

He crashed, of course, which is not to say he lost hope then or later. No doctor ever withdrew the doom, but no doctor ever said *Get ready now.* They said *We can manage this pain.* With a morphine pump that didn't or that baffled his mind. They said *Radiation can reduce the malignancy and make you more comfortable.* With five weeks of treatments that consumed his last days and energy. They said *It could be months; it could be five years.* With a remote hope we clutched close. They said the truth as they knew it, but they were all wrong. (*What did you learn from Gary's illness?* I asked Dr. Mabry months later. *That sometimes we don't know as much as we think.*)

So it was as though Gary disappeared for three months and then was gone. He was a very private man, and a man who had defied death before. He allowed only our family, and Mark and Barb, with us while we waited: waited for the turn, waited for his strength, waited for the wonder drugs, waited for the radiation, waited for a night's sleep. He didn't see his colleagues. He didn't see his best friends who lived out of town. He didn't see Andrea or Kerry, who were far away. He almost didn't see his mother, his brother, Lance. *Wait,* he said.

Liz wouldn't. She wanted to see for herself. And she saw Gary, one Sunday, clear in mind because his pain was high. She also saw that he was dying. Liz did not speak these words to me, nor I to her as we walked once—at my exhausted, distraught pace—around the block. Ian stayed with his father, attending with the tenderness he had been trying out, offering up, for only a few post-rebel years. Scratch the tattoos, Ian bled love. That weekend Gary needed both Ian's gentleness and strength, because a trial drug almost paralyzed his legs.

Mine flew around the block; words exploded; fears

poured. *So fast:* unshockable Liz was shaken, which unleashed the dilemma ripping me. Long distance I had poured out to Andrea and Kerry, but always I said to them, as he wanted, *Wait*. Now I could say, *I don't want to see it but I do! If he's having a bad day, I can't worsen it with 'We can't wait. You have things you want and need to do.' If he's having a good day, how can I spoil it?*

Liz could not answer the unanswerable, but she became a new Liz for me, a Liz I needed. She cut through what confusion she could—and she bore her witness to Gary's brother, Brent, in California. Gary had held onto managing the financial affairs of his invalid mother, in a Tennessee nursing home, and I could not say to him *You must pass this on.* Liz said, "They are a family. Brent is a man. This is not your job." And so, sensibly, she went home and called Brent. She also said to him, as I learned later, "If you want to see him, come now."

Mythic Time

Bolus. It means lump, also a soft pill. In the age of morphine pumped directly into the body in a steady stream, it means a hit, the extra jolt a patient push-buttons when the stream is too shallow for the pain. The pumps are battery-operated, programmed by the anaesthesiologist's prescription, delivering the liquid relief in a set amount and specifying the bolus dose and interval—three per hour, say. Push for four: nothing.

Gary's pump was never right. Nor were he and morphine. He wrestled with the god of dreams and sleep and vision and oblivion for two months, but the balance never came. He could be drowsy and out, agitated and obsessive, mobile and delusional, alert and on the cusp of pain. But he could never be steady for long, fully himself and truly pain-free. More than a modest visitation from Morpheus, and Gary was fellow-traveler to another plane.

"It's his system," said Dr. Henry, the gentlest member of Team Pain. "He's always been this way. Only now we know it." Who could have known? This was the man who took cheerful acid trips every weekend for months (before my time), who held his bourbon better than the best, whose legendary martinis worked their way into his obituary, who treated hard-core heroin addicts and understood narcotics better than consulting psychiatrists.

Chemical mysteries fascinated him, but now he was inside one. And attached to one. What crutch or pleasure do you love having near you? A cup of coffee? Chocolates? Aspirin? Vodka? Cigarettes? The refrigerator? Well, now imagine being wired to it. It is you. You can't get out of bed in the middle of the night and stumble to the bathroom, because there it is, on the bedside table, yanking you back. You never know when it will malfunction and beep alarmingly—even three times in one night, drawing the home nurses out of their beds and quickly to yours. You cannot mentally master, because of the very substance it pumps, the complicated ritual of changing batteries, replacing empty drug bags, resetting codes. You like to take it apart, though, when it has floated you to secretive paranoia—unwinding all its extra wires, winding them back, these life lines, these fate threads. Gary bore always with him a talisman, surgically attached, blessing, burden.

I was its operator. The Sunday night after Liz and Ian left, Gary lay down for bed in pain, and I sat for the night on the floor beside him, where I could see the clock and push the bolus button every five minutes. It was a ridiculous regimen, the latest in a series of trial-and-error drug programmings decided by physicians over the phone. Finally that day I had typed out an entire chronology of these stabs at pain management. No one was keeping track. Even I was getting confused. More, though, I was wrathful. Now I was armed with paper, determined to wave my weapon of anal recordkeeping (right down to the pedantic term *boli*) at *someone*.

Sleep deprivation. As if pain, fear, heartbreak, and morphine weren't enough to drag us deep into altered states, not sleeping did. Isn't it curious that trance states, waking dreams, visit precisely because humans do not close their eyes, because they do not allow the mind's eye to open in sleep? I did not know what wakefulness was doing to me. It was my morphine, my small taste of Gary's plane. For days at a time, he never slept more than two or three hours continuously, and neither did I. I had no visions, no wondrous revelations; but I was possessed.

The next morning we went to the hospital by ambulance, because Gary's legs still wouldn't work. The pump had nothing to do with the paralysis, caused by an injected anaesthetic that decided to flow down, not up toward the cancer. Meanwhile the pump was set far too low, with its miniscule five-minute boluses. Yet Gary had slept fairly well through my vigil and the pain paradox was in play: he was alert because he hurt. He bore with dignity being borne by EMTs. He joked with the oncology nurses about not being able to stay away. He sat up in his bed not looking like a desperately ill, wasting man worn to the bone and into the brain with weeks of drug changes.

But I knew. I thrust my paper history at the nurse, who looked properly awed and listened patiently as I ranted about the multiple Oz anaesthesiologists controlling Gary from behind the curtain. She vanished with my list. I perched on the boxy wall heater beside Gary's bed, clutching another copy, waiting for Dr. X, colleague and designated substitute for kind Dr. Henry, who was away. X arrived. To this day I do not remember his name. Or care to. Black hair, not young or old, slight accent, sure of himself, nice enough, clueless. He breezed in as if he were in a flu ward. He stood at the foot of the bed, tilted Gary's chart upward, let it fall, and asked him where he hurt. What was the pain like. And when did it start?

As Gary slowly got out partial answers—he could do nothing quickly that day, no matter how conscious—X was on to another irrelevant question. I interjected when Gary was really struggling. Then I had had it. Dr. X, puffed with professionalism, was so far from knowing what was happening and why we were there that he hadn't even left Kansas yet. Oh, but wait. He was being paged. Now he was dialing from Gary's bedside phone. We sat. He listened. It could have been Mrs. X. But whoever the mystery pager was, the good doctor decided he might as well consult about Gary and commenced sharing the wealth of information he had just gathered—all wrong. I couldn't hear everything he said, however, because a woman somewhere nearby was screaming, *Get out of here! Just get out of here NOW! GET OUT!* When she paused for breath, I was able to hear a bug-eyed X explain meekly into the phone, "Uh, that is his wife."

And so it was. I woke to realize the shrieking woman was I. Death and telephones: twice now the catalysts for flying leaps out of consciousness. The body does, sometimes, what it must. You find out later.

Dr. X, unfortunately, didn't get to get out. He had to wait, while I, back in my body with mad-woman license, asked a few questions of my own. *Can't you see that this man is very ill and in pain? Do you even know what his diagnosis is? Why are you making* HIM *tell his whole history when he's already done it and done it and done it. There's a chart, a* CHART. *Did you think about reading it?!* I also waved The List.

Utterly cowed, Dr. X mumbled that he liked for patients to talk. *Not when they have mesothelioma and have been on a morphine pump for two months!*

Soon we were calm, though, and getting to the business of helping Gary, when another physician rushed into the room. The ear on the other end of the phone, it turned out, belonged to the head of the pain practice. He clearly expected a still-raging virago. There I placidly sat, talking about *boli.* His face was a study.

Both men spoke thoughtfully, respectfully, and receptively with Gary and with me. When they left, I was ashamed. I had lost it. I was hysterical. I shouted. I brought the big honcho doctor running. Worst of all, I had violated one of my rules, a pledge made because I knew Gary so well: Don't get between him and his doctors. I was shaken and sorry, I said so, and I meant it. "You were," Gary said with finality, "exactly appropriate."

Shifting Time

Gary could get in physicians' faces. That day, he simply couldn't summon the energy. In this illness, *in extremis*, almost no truism about his behavior (or about mine) held, and yet, paradoxically, essence remained adamantine. I have never seen, nor may I ever again, a human being with so much mental strength while mentally besieged and bodily battered. Gary could swing between absolute lucidity and deep dementia; he could also know it was happening. Calmly once he said, "I think the pump is set too high. I am looking at my hand and watching it rot." His morphine madness also oscillated as wildly between the horrifying and the hilarious. Rot wasn't his whole vision. He took me, one night, on a rocket ride on the couch (insisting I handle the invisible joystick), as gleeful as a ten-year-old.

He never stayed in space, though, and what I knew—though strangers could not see it—was that Gary was always, somewhere, Gary, and always, somehow, aware. A hospice team came once, just to meet us before hospice was authorized. Gary was not in much pain that day and was mobile; also loose, drifting. He sat beside me on the couch, facing a nurse in the rocker and a very large social worker wedged into a small chair chosen to fit me. She talked most, explaining, asking questions, answering them. Gary's eyes were roaming all about. He got up, sat down again. Whatever the discussion, I spoke to and with him as I always had. I sat there as a *we*, including him, asking for his opinions, doing so seriously—and knowing how it looked. Gary was somewhere else. The social worker came around to time. Six months, she explained. Hospice was only for the last six months. Gary was on his feet, agitated, talking loud, not clear, exiting fast to the bedroom. The social worker (keen, kindly, realistic, *and* touchyfeely, as the family came to know) didn't hesitate. She got it before I did. "I'm going to explain," she announced. What, I wasn't sure, but down the hall she went. The nurse looked at me with compassion, "It must be hard for you, seeing him like this."

In the bedroom doorway, I listened as the straight-arrow young woman said her piece to Gary, who was sitting up like a king in bed: She was only talking about the medical rules. She didn't know Gary's prognosis—that was Dr. Mabry's realm—and she did not mean he had six months or less to live. She wanted to be very clear. Gary said nothing. I showed them out and went back to him. He had only one thing to say about the whole episode, one professional's sincere but morphined appreciation of another: "I like that fat girl."

Oh, yes, it was hard seeing him like this, but the nurse didn't see what I did.

Of course Gary's wrath and testy pride were not, as you have probably suspected, reserved for outsiders. He could be a bad patient with the ones who really had to take it: me and Kristy. Gary always hated having food pushed on him. It was my job now. What fun. Or he could complain that he *would* drink more fluids if only he had certain odd juices which I did my best to find, only to be accused of buying the wrong ones on purpose. Or he would forget when he had taken what medication, or mix up the regimen, and proceed to pontificate about all things medicinal, in general and in particular to his treatment. Kristy came in from one of these lecture-spats with his scheduled medicine still in her hand. She was steaming (he was outside on the deck, busy meandering): "I know he's sick and the morphine messes up his mind and I shouldn't try to argue and I shouldn't let it get to me and I'm being petty, but once, just once, I want to *be right and win.*" Amen, daughter.

The sharp mind that feared its dulling could turn the blade against us.

Only in flashes. Tenderness was the real truth of that time. Gary and I clung together in desperation and in solace. Far from wanting me not to hover, he could not stand our tether being cut. We were much alone. Our friends worried about it. The home health nurse worried about it. Sometimes I worried about it. And yet whenever I had any time away—to my own doctor, to the pharmacy—I panicked to return. And though we could not be normal, though we could not even press ourselves hard together because of pain, every moment was not agony. We were together. Our acts were new, but together. Bathing him. Dressing him. Driving to radiation. Smoothing on the cream that soothed the burning from radiation. Moving slowly, slowly. Marking one more day. Sitting each evening, like any couple might, in our living room until the longed-for moment arrived. Gary was ready for bed. We lay down on our backs, sides touching, heads together, hands clasped. So tired, so desperate, so hopeless, so still. We slept. Not forever, not even for long, but we slept.

Inexorable Time

Here is how I learned to walk in the world, at the

last, without weeping. It is useful to know: Recite yourself into the physical. Suppose you're in the drug store; tears well. Dark glasses aren't enough. Recite. *I am in the greeting card aisle. I am walking down the right side. My hand is lifting to adjust my glasses. I see detergent ahead. My feet are stepping right, left, right.* Into my body. Out of my mind.

Gary was so awfully, wonderfully in and out of his. Such scenes. Something was coming. Something had to come. But what? When? People came.

His brother and mother came. Brent an even wirier version of Gary, nine years older, black-haired still, taciturn, gravel-voiced, infinitely loyal, a bedrock person. Lama, "Mammaw" to all, nearly blind, traveling arduously when she thought all her travel over, to see her baby, in shadow. Gary was furious (*It's too soon! I'll be stronger!*), but he got over it. He was a master of rising to occasions. Few saw the falls.

So we had a visit. Absolutely nothing was ordinary, but most unusual was that we ignored it. I, who had not cooked a meal in weeks, laid the table with a roast. Gary brought a pillow to his chair, determined to sit with us. We assembled before the television, though no one watched. Gary carried on lucid conversations that veered suddenly into snot discussions, caught himself, made Brent laugh. We left the house for radiation, and Brent packed up his mother's financial records.

The home health nurse came. The mesothelioma was advancing, not retreating, so Mabry had her begin interferon shots. Gary went back to bed; Brent and Mammaw sat in ear shot; they heard her say, "You cannot do this alone much longer." Brent said before they left for Tennessee, "Did you hear her?"

Kristy came, and the taxi driver didn't. We were trying

morphine in pills, too, to find some solution, some balance to the trials of the pump. Kristy watched her father and watched me. She saw him smoking again and wandering. She saw him nodding whenever he sat. She saw me cautioning him, rubbing out glowing ashes. She was firm: "You have let him be in charge long enough. We have to take his cigarettes away. Hide them." I did, and after she left, I hid the morphine tablets too. I found him with all his pill bottles open, meticulously marking X's all over our complicated daily drug sheet.

He wanted cigarettes. More, Gary did not want to be a person whose cigarettes were confiscated. Late at night, with intense effort, garbled but eloquent, he said, "I have put up with a lot. I have been treated like a child. I can do almost nothing. I don't know how much longer I want to be half-dead. Cigarettes are not killing me," and he got dressed in jeans and black jacket, with the pump inside, and called a taxi.

I was amazed he found the number. He dialed. He said, "Do you know where I am?"

I love this question still. I think it is what everyone who calls a taxi really wants to ask. It terrified me too. He did give his address. I sat next to him while he waited. "What will you do, Gary, if the pump begins to squeal, if it stops pumping, if you can't stop the pain?" This proud, stubborn man. I had so little hope. This proud, stubborn man full of surprises. He took off his jacket. He looked at me, utterly naked and aware and unangry, and he stayed at home, not smoking.

A Gorgon came. I was beyond tired. Sometimes in the night Gary rose from bed without me. I would wake, frenzied, and rush to find him. This night he looked up as I came into the living room. Again, the pump. How many times had I found him like this, how many times that I did not even know had he opened it, examined it, worried it, tried to unravel its secrets? He said, with the monstrous succor spread out beside him, "You have no idea how many Medusa wires are in here." I delivered him of the pump. I detached it and bandaged his body. I did not call a nurse or a doctor to ask permission. If my husband thought he was metaphorically, mythologically united to Medusa, it was time to wield the sword.

The doctor came, and hospice didn't. Dr. Mabry was making a house call. After sixteen years, it surprised me and excited Gary. He stood watch outside and shouted "Hey!" at cars. I stood watch over Gary. When Dr. Mabry finally turned into the drive, Gary turned toward the house, said "Taurus," and retreated to his recliner. He was not impressed. Being "not impressed" was one of Mabry's favorite terms, and often we were glad for it. This wry and witty man was never impressed with conclusions made on scanty or anecdotal evidence. That day he was observing first-person but also being the human being who had grown to middle-age along with a patient he cared for more than he could admit.

So he was impressed, as I related it, with Gary's Medusa metaphor. He was jokingly impressed with finding *The New York Review of Books* on the table, not the *National Enquirer.* He laughed out loud when I noted the *Enquirer* was radiation waiting-room fare, along with Gary's and my two favorites, *Hogs Today* and *Pork.* And he was apparently impressed when Gary put together whole paragraphs of talk, asking when he was going to be able to go water skiing with the family—a sport that, unknown to Dr. Mabry, was totally unknown to the family.

Oh, he knew Gary was in a bad way. He saw clinical evidence of decline (a drooping eyelid: "Horner's syndrome") that I couldn't interpret. But he also saw a man sitting up in a recliner, making mythic analogies, laughing with his wife, longing to water ski. We discussed oral medication and then said good-bye.

Gary wandered the house all night. In the morning I called the social worker about hospice, about someone to help me care, to help us both rest. She would get me a list of independent "sitters." I didn't understand. Didn't hospice do this? "You see," she said apologetically, who should be glad, "we can't. Dr. Mabry didn't say 'Six months.'"

Mark and Barb came. It was Saturday. Lance was due that night from California. He had been waiting for me to say *now*, and finally I had known now was here, no matter how much Gary improved. I needed Lance's help, and it was only hours away. A real action, a change, hold on.

I couldn't. All the night before, Gary had waked me. Without the pump, but still morphine mad, he had become obsessed with showering, once locking himself in our bathroom while I panicked that he had fallen into the deep sunken tub. Now I had locked that bath permanently. This night, though, he wasn't even leaving the bed. *Hello, hello,* I would hear, as though he were calling to me from a distance—which of course he was. And he would talk, repetitively, "perseverating," a word he taught me about psychotic behavior. He had something to tell me. It wasn't mad. *I love you, I love you, I love you, I love you, I love you, I love you, I love you, I love you, I love you.*

Oh, my love, let me sleep. He couldn't. In the

morning, he was busy. Busy and talkative. I had to call a pharmacist, and without warning he grabbed the receiver, fighting me for it. I could not believe his strength. I hung up, and Gary docilely seemed to forget the phone.

Except that he began to discuss his many medicines, which I was trying to give him, and to notate the check-off list, which I was trying to prevent. With great authority, he told me that drug X did this and that and was in the class of Y, but Z did such and so and was . . .

And I said, "No, Z does this and that."

And he loftily, patiently said, "Yes, well, X does this and that and A also is one of the . . . "

I said, "No, X does *not.*"

He said.

I said.

He said.

I screamed. "Shut up! Shut up! You don't know what you're talking about! You are *wrong.* Wrong! You do not know *anything.*"

We breathed in the shocked silence. He shut up, like a child. He was not a child. I went to another room and called Mark and Barb: *I screamed at Gary. I attacked him. It's absurd, he's suffering, this is what I've come to, and I can not do this to him.*

They arrived in minutes. I have never felt so physically explosive in my life. I do not even remember whether Barb and I walked in Roselawn. We must have. Around the block wasn't long enough. I couldn't move fast enough. We almost ran. I needed air. I needed to spew words. I, bone tired, blood tired, needed to exhaust myself. She listened, she paced me, she said she would have screamed long ago. It was enough; now I needed home.

Twice Mark stayed with Gary while I was away. The first time Gary needed Mark's strong presence but stayed secreted in the bedroom. This time Gary walked amiably about with his friend, secreted in his own world. He was whimsical Gary now whimsied far beyond us. Mark observed (a psychologist fascinated in spite of himself): "He picked up kindling and puffed on it. The connections are there." Gary smiled serenely. But of course.

Lance came. Once again, Gary pulled it together. He greeted Lance as himself, spectral-thin and halting, but himself. Lance sobbed in the garage. Not a skinny kid in a graveyard; twenty-seven and six feet tall; a Wittgenstein scholar, Zen student, blazing guitar player; still undone.

Then our marathon began. We did not know how to manage the new morphine. Was Gary taking too much? Was it causing the bizarre episodes? How could he survive if he ate nothing, if he never slept? When Gary unpredictably refused to swallow pills, how long before the searing pain would return? Nothing but death terrified me more. No. That pain, and watching it, was worse.

How can I tell you that Gary also was hilarious? That Lance and I now (and Kristy before) could laugh hysterically? I can tell you because it is the truth. A funny man is a funny man.

Lance's first role was to let me rest. He stretched his solid length out on the floor in Gary's and my bedroom; I lay on the futon in Gary's study, hiding, door locked; Gary bobbed in and out of bed, wanting me. He yielded to Lance's diversion of watching television. They settled together in the living room,

Gary ensconced in his usual chair while Lance switched between channels: "What do you want to watch?" Gary shifted back in the recliner: "Who gives a shit?"

After sufficient entertainment, he returned to the bedroom and industriously flossed between his toes.

He lay down again but was bull-dog determined. "Where's your mother?" he asked Lance.

Lance, by now expecting confusion and jet-lagged himself, heard Gary wrong. "She's gone back to Tennessee," Lance reminded him.

Gary set his stepson straight, with scathing pity: "Lance, your mother is *Ellen*. *My* mother is in Tennessee."

He wanted to go into our bath. Lance used the factual, nonexplanatory technique: "We can't. The door is locked."

"Oh!" said Gary. A pause, a solution. "Well, then, let's break it down." Lance diverted him during the battering-ram search.

Finally Gary found me, or found the other locked door. Lance did his best at another fake-out, but I emerged. "It's no good, Lance. Back to my bed." I walked toward Gary's side of the bed, intending to help him fix the ritual pillows that propped him away from some pain. I found my hand firmly grasped; Gary took me to my side of the bed and made sure I was prone.

It didn't last. Later, all three of us gathered in the TV room, but Gary wasn't interested. He stood up. "What's that?" he asked, opening his robe, pulling out the waistband of his underwear, pointing inside. I told him. He snapped the band back. "Funny looking, isn't it?" Point taken.

Finally, though, words failed him. He wanted desperately to tell me something, but it came out *petunias* or, sometimes, *pants. Petunias, petunias, petunias, pants!* He brushed his hair with his shoe.

What was happening? He was not ready for hospice. When would he come back?

Gary's fat girl was as good as he thought. She came to me and Lance. She sat in the same small chair and listened while we talked about how much Gary shifted from himself to Other, talked about holding on, talked about waiting and watching. "If you wait," she asked, not pressuring, "what will that accomplish? Won't it be just that much harder, maybe in the middle of the night, maybe in crisis?"

We called the doctor, rolled Gary in his office chair to the car, and went to the hospital. It was Monday.

The security guards came, and the CAT scan didn't. This is so hard. This is too much. He still has so far to go but so little time and the point is: He did come back. Here are the horrors but flat.

He thought I was leaving and cried *If you go, I'll die!* He knew that hospital.

Dr. Mabry said *We need to find out if it is in his brain. But it will mean no medication for a while.*

Gary, 109 pounds now, could barely walk but fought the orderlies sent from radiology. They called security guards, who wrestled him to the gurney and tied him down. Absurd. Obscene.

Gary did not want his head in the machine. The technicians gave up and turned to me. I tried. Dr. Henry feared using anaesthesia. We tried again. Dr. Henry risked it; the image was made. No one sent it to Mabry, who was told every time he called, *They couldn't get the scan.*

We did not know this. We watched for Mabry
till late. Gary was quiet, so I went home to sleep.
Lance stayed. All night Gary raved, was excruciated,
could not stay in bed. A nurse said: *I am thinking it is
withdrawal.* Lance raved: *Stop this pain* NOW. The nurse
threatened him with security guards. He threatened
back: *If you do not call Dr. Mabry I am going to his house.*
They called. Lance called me at dawn. Gary roared in
the background. I came.

Gary, finally, was sedated. Mabry came into the
room and said: *We'll try one more time for the scan.* I
exploded. *Wasn't the image any good?* Now the mistake
was clear. Mabry apologized, rushed out, surely
exploded at someone else, saw the scan, said: *His brain
is clear. We can keep him sedated now. That is all.*
How long? *It could be days; it could be weeks.*

Kristy and Ian came. It was two days. I slept that
night in Gary's hospital room, a restive erratic night,
and the next day when his daughter and son arrived,
the miraculous happened. He was their father. Thick-
tongued, very very slow, but no petunias. He looked
at Kristy and said, "You've had a haircut," which she
had. He looked at me and said, "You look beautiful,"
which I didn't. He looked at Ian, and smiled.

Simple sentences. The burst of happiness they gave
me made me know I had despaired of any more. And
so had Gary. I saw his full knowledge in every intense
struggle to speak. He had been somewhere dark. It
was fundamentally important to say, simply, "I am
here, among you."

He pulled away again, or was pulled, but each of
us had our time. That night Kristy and Ian camped in
the room. Gary needed their quiet constancy, not the
nurse who shouted *Gary sweetie!* into his semicoma. In

the morning I discovered them still sleeping, wedged on chairs and cot in the dimness of his room. They raised up groggy, blinking, disheveled, children again. Suddenly I was looking back, way back, at van, tent, motel, all the close quarters we had shared. They went home to wander an empty house with Lance. *Rest came.* Gary did not stir. He lay on his back. I had forgotten until this moment: I wanted to wash his beautiful hair. I was obsessed with it. A last dignity, I suppose. I tried the hospital's waterless shampoo. I could not do it as I wanted. Suddenly I was foolish to myself. This did not matter. This was not it. What I wanted most was to lie with him, and I did.

Close against him in the narrow bed, head on his shoulder, I spoke. I told him not to worry, that all the things he had wanted would be done. I went through them. I know Gary. Closure counts. The very words, now, do not. Always, there are secrets. But you can know this: I spoke love. My love, his love, our love, a family's love. I drew him near; I set him free. We lay so still, so hopeless, so calm. We slept. I woke. Gary let go.

Space

Back to the ground, to Roselawn. I can't remember whether the funeral home or I called Mr. Britt about the plot. Even if I, he did not recognize me. The children and I set out through the gate to meet him. It was April, a glorious April. We were in one of our bravura, light mood swings. Suddenly, bluebirds—flying right across our path. A Gary emblem, we decreed, and laughed. From a distance, Wayne Britt, seasoned cemetery caretaker, watched us approaching, realized this was no family walk, and could not hide his stunned face: "I knew it was someone who lived here. But you." Yes. Surprise. Walk this ground or cruise it, round and round, year after year, it still can give out beneath your feet.

Common Space

Kristy, blessedly, had gone with me to the funeral home. The business of dying, like of all of modern life, has too many options. One plot or two? Metal casket or wood? And on and on and on. I bought two plots. "You did?," Liz later exclaimed, who had not. This was, perhaps, something practical that living by Roselawn had done for me, allowing me a choice not necessarily foreboding fate, as it had seemed for Liz, a widow at twenty-nine. I knew this dirt rectangle was, among all its other aching meanings, real estate—which might never be developed. Maybe I'm lying. Maybe I didn't think that then, or not only that. Anyway, I bought two.

The casket should have been easy but wasn't. Gary did not come from a cremation family. While a hater of funeral rigmarole, he nevertheless drew a line at heat reduction. "I know the process," he always said. "I just want to do it in a pine box." I could see his imp smile at the lawyer's office eight years earlier: "Put in 'burial as cheaply as possible.'" So Kristy and I had two goals: wood, cheap. They didn't coexist at Culley & Sons. Kristy bullied both me and the 'counselor' a bit, seeing we needed it. "Too expensive. What's in *this* room?" We found a metal one that wasn't hideous or astronomical. I wasn't sure. "Ellen," Kristy said, "Dad did not mean a mahogany-stained casket with satin bolsters that costs $9,000." The counselor had a nonwood sale.

Still, when we later got out the will and I rediscovered that the imp had prescribed in full "in a plain pine box, at as little expense as possible," I went into another paroxysm about penny wise and pine foolish. Ian this time gave me the metaphoric shake about literalness: "He thought pine was the *cheapest*. He's not upset."

The things we worry about when the object of worry is far beyond our cares. We did know exactly how we wanted the burial to be: separate from the memorial service, a simple family circle around the grave, a walk out the gate to the waiting coffin, no circuitous, showy hearse parade. The spot we'd chosen was not many yards from the house, in view of our other spot. As a family we'd not only had death practice in Roselawn, we were at home here. It's a truism that families come together for holidays, marriages, and deaths. Ours blurred boundaries somewhat—we walked off turkey dinners in a graveyard. We had done it just four months ago, all of us assembling in Tallahassee (not often the case in our extended, blended family with other parents elsewhere): Kristy, Lance, Ian and Stephanie (his girl friend of nine years), Andrea, Kerry, Gary, and I. Liz and the boys came for one day before Christmas. People, presents, and clothes everywhere; bathroom jams; cooking, eating, and drinking nonstop; people coming, people going, people disputing game rules; every single strong-willed individual getting along, having fun, and *knowing* it. It was a miracle.

It was a gift.

We felt it keenly when we were all together again,

minus one. Finally, Andrea and Kerry were with me. My two striking sisters were both managers, though one in academe and one in business, and formidable, no doubt, to those they managed — Andrea sophisticated and silver-haired, Kerry razor-minded under impossible white-blond curls — and yet so clearly southern, warm at the core. Vulnerable, in fact, and totally trusting in their different ways with my husband. Andrea, who never appeared to need support, leaned thankfully on Gary. Kerry, who lived solitary by choice, settled comfortably beside him to smoke and drink. Told *wait* so long, they would have only this good-bye to their brother-in-law. But they had had Christmas, the happy holiday for the history books.

So out the gate we went for the service, a long straggle of family and of course Mark and Barb. I looked toward the site. My fallen heart, so obsessed with creating ceremony Gary would not despise, fell deeper. There by the grave in which he already lay were unrequested funereal effects. First of all, two tight-black-suited mourners, feet apart, arms behind their backs, lips slipping about between solemnity and smile. Then rows of seats: spindly-legged folding chairs fancified with royal blue crushed velvet covers. Tacky, tacky, tacky. But I wasn't laughing. I was sick. In my state, all I could see was an affront — and a problem. Something had to be done.

It was. Ian, who'd not long ago been given Gary's guided tour of his home town, Memphis, observed: "A little touch of Elvis."

Perfect. Now I could picture Gary singing "That's All Right, Mama," skinny leg twitching. A Gary moment, definitely. Distress dispelled, I politely explained that the chairs (and suits) could be retired. We gathered round. Words were said, tears were shed. Lance sang, playing the guitar I'd given Gary for Christmas. Each of us gave Gary one last gift, a single flower. We went back through the gate, ate, drank, and shot basketballs in the driveway.

A few days later, Gary sang for his own service. A voice is only vibrations, but it isn't insubstantial. It is concrete. We hear it because it sets our own bodies vibrating. I think you know—those of you who can still play a voice long gone—that such vibrations are a presence more powerful than any photograph. Especially when the voice is rich, emotional, flexible, and singing songs brought out of itself. Gary was a spare man to look at. To hear him was another matter. Said a fellow singer-songwriter hearing him for the first time, "Some set of pipes."

So Gary's voice filled the Unitarian auditorium that day. It punctuated and permeated the eloquent, funny tributes from his friends, from Kristy, from Andrea, from his first wife, Pam. It sang his own words and others'. It led us in with Dylan's "One Too Many Mornings" and out with Hank Williams's "I'm So Lonesome I Could Cry." It reached back to graduate school weariness at "trying to make rhyme out of reason." It traveled his daily commute to a state mental hospital, past homeless drifters, arriving at his own self-admonition: "Driver, Don't Turn Your Eyes." A long time passed before I could hear that voice again.

This day, though, we all did what we had to do, steadied by the rituals of mourning. Isn't that what they're for—steadiness, busyness—as well as for homage? The wake, continued at home and in

Roselawn, we called a celebration, which it was. And like any performance and party, it had given us all much to do. At home, though, I passed through the gathering like a sleepwalker, a solid spectre, an alien in glass. I was there and nowhere near. Oh, I talked with people. I was glad to see friends from far away. I heard their memories of Gary. *(Come to think of it,* one of his old friends teased, *I've known Gary longer than you have.* Quite true, but *You haven't slept with him as long.)* Surely some withdrew to weep, but mostly people did what Gary would have wanted: reminisced and laughed, wandered back to the grave, drank gallons, ate tons. I watched, remote but grateful, as Andrea and Kerry worked like frenzied caterers, then rested, then tried to give me food. I couldn't eat. I couldn't sit. I moved my bubble from room to room, outside to in. I drank white wine. I never got drunk. I never cried. I said good-bye to friends who did. By midnight all were gone.

I closed the door to our bedroom, lay down, and waited for blackness. The house quieted. Everyone slept. The blackness wouldn't come. I took half of the smallest Valium, enough to make me sleep eight hours. The blackness wouldn't come. Now I know that wine, no food, and Valium were indeed working in me, but I didn't know it then. I felt completely in control, and I knew what I had to do. In the short satin robe Kerry had brought me, barefoot, out the glass doors I went. Across the yard, through the gate, past the bluebird box, down the path, to the grave. I lay full-length on the fresh red clay and, like Liz in the chapel, lost it. Somewhere far away, sober Ellen knew this was a bit much, but she wasn't in charge. This grit, these tears, the glass woman needed them.

Here is the reason I knew to write, "Of the abyss inside Liz, I could only guess." No guessing now.

Empty Space

Gary sang in Roselawn once, at my father's burial. Why did I delay telling? It irritated me, for one. Its truth belongs here, for another. I was that day, to use a friend's phrase, "a nerve with hair." All my sorrow had clenched to tension. That's no excuse for wishing Gary wouldn't bring his guitar to graveside and sing "I'm So Lonesome I Could Cry." There is no excuse for that shameful solipsism. My taut nerves are the only *reason* I can find, though. Because no one sang that song like Gary. No one. If you are imagining a maudlin Elvis version, don't. Gary sang it pure—straight, simple, letting the melody do its lonesome work—which is why it moved.

Nevertheless, my brittle selfishness that day shut my ears. I knew how I was supposed to feel as Gary ended our ceremony—*And as I wonder where you are, I'm so lonesome I could cry*—but I felt only awkwardness: the cumbersome guitar case, the tuning, the solo performance in the open air. Then it got worse. We had walked no more than a few feet from the grave when Gary stopped and began sobbing. What was going on with him? Of course I felt sympathy, but this was so unlike reserved, undramatic Gary. Kerry, Andrea, and Liz left us alone. My face must have been asking some impatient wifely questions: *What does this mean? Why are you breaking down now when you didn't for mother or Gordon?*

"That's what he's been doing," Gary said, still crying. "For seven years, that's what he's been doing—

wondering where she is." Open your ears, Ellen; open your eyes. Gary saw into the heart of grief. I knew he was right then. I have lived it now.

For all the ache and loss of my parents' and brother's deaths—for their loss of glorious life, for my loss of theirs—the absence of Gary was a pit like no other. A crack in the earth, a fissure. My father dropped in when mother died and never climbed out. *I wonder where you are.* It is not that I puzzled over the place Gary had gone, whether to heaven or a spirit space or into Roselawn's clay, but that wind blew through me. Bereft, body of my body robbed, seized, torn away. What has happened? What is this hole? Where is my other? How am I here and he not? Wonderment of *being*, so changed.

Acting, doing, helps, as I know it did for my father too, but routine is no refuge. There the hole gapes most. It blindsides you at the most banal moments. In the cereal aisle at the grocery, say: never again to need Toasted Nutty Somethings. Andrea and Lance stayed behind with me for a while, Lance into midsummer. They tolerated my falling disproportionately apart over broken appliances and a baby snake under my bed. (Lance and I, equals in squeamishness, flushed it into a corner and shot at it with Raid. Once again: poof. Empty corner, no snake, not even a carcass under the carpet.) We weren't unremittingly morose. You can't squirt snakes with bug spray and not laugh. Yet everywhere that hole, gaping and heavy. I dragged it through all the business of death, through the endless lists Lance and I made, through the paperwork and legalities and phone calls and courthouse trips. Through visits from friends and invitations to lunch. Then Lance was gone, and I alone with it. *I've never seen a night so long, when time goes crawlin' by.*

I knew this before I could say it: In grief, an absence is a presence. In my bed, for the first days after Gary's death, it was palpable. His energy vibrated beside me. I know this is true, because it left. I looked for him everywhere. On his birthday in the summer, two bluebirds sat on the basketball backboard. His emblem! Then I rounded the garage to the pool pump, where the long shed skin of a snake greeted me. Romanticism deflated. More appropriate, really, this emblem of passage (this earth god of sexual creation and death), though less lovely. Oh, I was no ghost summoner. Getting out the Ouija board was my sign to cork the wine bottle. I wanted him. That was all. A want. I breathed him in his unwashed jeans for months. Even his handwriting pained me.

Dream Space

September. I am walking at night, down the side of a desolate highway. The unlighted road where I walk is the only landscape, dream as close shot. A terrific gale is blowing, terrific. The wind blasts straight at me—but not at my face. For I am walking, must walk, backward. Only this way can I make any progress, but every step is arduous. I am bent by this wind into a curve. I rest against its force, bracing myself, to lift and drag each foot. Slow motion, slow as moving through oily air.

I am in danger too. Only the roadside white line can save me. My whole focus, undivided, unwavering, must be on that line. If I wander over the line onto the road—and I do, for oh the physical strain to keep upright—I will be killed by the speeding cars whose headlights come at me like comets. Now! Another! Too close—almost gone! Concentrate.

Concentrate. Watch the line. Lift, drag, lift.
I wake. The divination comes to me whole. The only way I can go forward now is not to look ahead and to walk a narrow line. If I do not, I am gone.

Light

Oh, I wallowed. I wept. Howled, really, alone at night. Yet I can say, curiously (and you may disbelieve), that what I was feeling was not self-pity. Not often. Sorrow, not sorry for myself. Grief is a physical condition, a pain as visceral as any wound.

Dawning Light

I understood something, though it could not stop the bleeding: The reason such a loss seems so hopeless, hurts so extravagantly, is love. The only way not to risk such pain is never to know the love. And who would risk that? Not I. Not Kristy or Ian or Gary's mother or my father or Liz. I could not be inside their separate aches, nor they in mine, but all had one core.

I have lucid dreams, dreams in which I know I'm dreaming. I had lucid love too. Gary and I were together for twenty-two years, not by any means all easy, not by any means all blissful. Often, I thought we would not last. But long before he died, here is where I had arrived: We are having a fight. We are speaking meanly. I am flinging about dramatically. He is digging his heels into the center of the earth. I am thinking he is an intolerant ass. I would like him to dissolve into a puddle and go down a drain. I would like to *do* the dissolving. I am fully in the grip of fury and also quite beyond it. I am thinking, *This will pass. We are blowing*

*up and will cool off and everything will be fine. I will be
with this man as long as he wants me, and he does.*

I don't think absolute love is an achievement. I feel
no arrogant pride. It is a gift. It does take time, and
space, and finally births light. Yet lucid or not, I was
still a pill on a regular basis. Gary too, even in deathly
illness. Once when he was irascible, accusatory, and
dismissive of my complete efforts to help him, Kristy
watched in disbelief as I did not even defend myself.
Alone later, she said to me, "You are a saint." Oh, no,
not at all. I take no credit. In ordinary life, Gary would
have gotten his own back—or worse. But this was not
ordinary life. This was life looking death in the eye.

And Gary knew. Kristy did not hear him say to me
one afternoon, quietly and simply, "Don't think I don't
know what you're doing for me. I would be dead."

For me, nothing was ever so emotionally and
physically arduous as caring for a fatally suffering
man every minute of every day. Nothing was ever
easier. It was not will. It was not martyrdom. How can
I say this simply? I did not have to try. I was watching
someone lose life. I was watching a being who soon
would lose being, and I would have given mine for
his. You who have been there know. Pettiness drops
away. I know I will never again be such a good person,
but I am forever a different one.

Wayne Britt came to work at Roselawn fourteen
years ago. He wears a diamond ear stud. He owns
a Harley. I knew none of this until recently, when I
stopped him to talk about a map, and talked about
the ground where we stood. He started by mowing,
cleaning, tending as his men do now—and watching.
"I would go home to my wife and say, 'I can't do this.'
She said, 'Yes, you can.' So much suffering, so much

love. I never wanted to work here. But after this, it's like the man said. You just try to do right by people."

Traveling Light

Heel-to-toe time, Andrea calls it. Everyone who survives grief does it the same way: one foot in front of the other. Just keep moving. Do. I accepted every invitation. I worked as soon as I could. Either do or dissolve, do or explode. Because only in action were the obsessive thoughts stilled for a moment—the endless round of scenes and voices, a tornado of thought swirling in my skull.

Almost a year and a half passed. I went to Scotland with Andrea, a huge trip for me, my first time abroad in twenty years. We traveled well together. We had adventures. We loved it. I had gotten far, far away, and when I came home, Gary still wasn't here. The voices were, the scenes were. I hadn't expected this. The tornado swelled and blackened and spun faster, until working with Peggy one night—overworked, too much work for me alone, and no Gary to say, "Stop!"—I couldn't keep the storm inside. I heard its incoherence whistling out, past my friend's worried face. Alone later, wild, I knew I was a beast cornered at the abyss. I called my doctor.

If you think therapy (or medication) is a prosaic modern response to an age-old problem—too bad. Watch the grieving ones you love. And you who are grieving, watch yourself. Two years may pass, but watch. Watch your storms. Watch your dreams. Watch your emptiness, calling you to rest.

Move. Heel-to-toe. You can look back. You won't forever. Take what enters your path. Wonder of wonders, new love crossed mine. Keep walking. You won't have a destination. You'll find yourself in a new place.

I look at my path: Roselawn. My walking place, my inescapable landscape, my quotidian kept winding me past death. I cannot say that these speaking stones, these reminders of others' loss and sorrow, made mine any easier. That is intellectual. But the seasons of Roselawn, the steps through it, the encounters in it, have. It is a private and precious world to me now, though shared, always shared.

I look back at Gary's black dance. When he saw those circling dancers, and for long after, I felt the unspeakable chill under the vision. Not now. Gary was gazing out from his home, which happens to be here: a verdant, peaceful place holding lives that have ended, drawing those that go on. Gordon's wedding to his funeral: the first circle of Roselawn in my life. The second: moving to the cemetery's edge. Not yet the last: laying down my love. I am still here, he was and is here, we all are here by accident. Sometimes accidents define.

This is a book about a cemetery. This is a book about steps. This is a book about circles and cycles and winding roads. This is a book about facing backward and forward and backward and forward. This is a book about death. This is a book about life. This is a book of love.

CHAPTER 7

Again

The story has gone on quite long enough, don't you think? I do. But then life doesn't know a thing about neat endings.

Two years after Gary's death, Kerry conquered her fear of flying to visit me for a long vacation. She came smiling out of the gate clutching her lucky stuffed toy—two-martini brave, tall, blond, big-boned, a head-turner. We crammed a lot into ten days. She flew home to Virginia safe; within days was at the emergency room with stomach pains; within six months was dead of colon cancer. Our blue-eyed baby sister.

Hers was the death I couldn't rise to. Hers was the death Andrea bore. Hers is the memory I can't yet build. I have time, though, and space, for the plot in Roselawn has lengthened once more. Kerry, always contrary, reversed our mourning. Her huge good-bye was first, in Virginia, where friends and colleagues jammed the chapel and spilled out its doors. Her family farewell followed, months later.

Summer again. As hot a day as dad's burial, a day indeed for ashes. I like to think, though, about the ashes that aren't sealed under Roselawn's clay. For not all of Kerry is here. Like mother, she sought the sea. Well, not exactly like mother. Mother didn't have her ashes sent out through the tides in a plastic pink alligator. You had to be there. You had to love crazy Kerry. All of Kerry's Virginia Beach buddies, commemorative drinks in hand, were and did. So some of Kerry's ashes are now a salty mingle with mother's. The rest we circled on that sunny day, our circle both diminished and expanded. Everything changes. Stephen stood beside me, pressing my hand while I tried to speak. My father's nephew and his wife—re-entering our lives after decades of absence—unexpectedly, wonderfully, filled out the ring.

I never knew Kerry had chosen Roselawn, but I should have. Her home was in Virginia; her family is here. She knew the feel of this place too, its curving paths, its slopes, its giant oaks. One of Kerry's oldest friends has not healed well. She is suffering, long and hard. "Come here," I say to her. "Come see this solid place. You do not know what being here may do for you." I know.

I longed for death and fell in love.

I lost that love and bled again.

I planned my death and did not do it.

No, I walked. I walked and stumbled and walked and ran and fell and rose once more.

And now I lay me down to roll. I am at the top of the grass-scratchy hill. I am looking at the milky sky. I push off and roll once, twice, more, bumping clumsily, laughing, disoriented, eyes open, eyes closed, getting a rhythm, arching now, whipping down, fish flopping down, rolling, rolling, rolling down, and when I stop the whole world spins, I am dizzy, I am sick, I am breathing, I am smiling, I am holding on until the streaking world slows, rights itself, shows me again this grass, these trees, these stones, these roads I know so well.

Here, I have made what monument I could.

About Ellen Ashdown

Ellen Ashdown is a writer now living at St. George Island, Florida. A Florida Fiction Fellow, she has published feature articles on art, dance, and education in regional and national magazines. She holds a Ph.D. in English from the University of Florida, is Phi Beta Kappa, a former dancer, and a writer for major textbook publishers, advertising agencies, and universities.

Her articles include feature stories on Suzanne Farrell, George Balanchine's muse and New York

City Ballet prima ballerina, and on Jawole Zollar, founder and artistic director of Urban Bush Women dance troupe. She wrote and edited two magazines for Florida State University: *Dance FSU* and *Comm Connections.*

Ellen has been a free-lance creative director for regional advertising agencies, creating all-media campaigns (print, radio, TV, electronic tie-ins) for a broad variety of clients, including telecommunications, banks, hospitals, retailers, state of Florida agencies, and numerous Florida State University divisions.

As both a former college professor (English and interdisciplinary Humanities) and a modern dancer (performing with the company Avodah, now based in New York, and in Florida State University productions as a guest artist), Ellen has deep interests in the life of the imagination and the interconnections of the arts.